For Shirley Shugart

For,

Fr. "Hal"

KITCHEN-TABLE
CHRISTIANITY

KITCHEN-TABLE CHRISTIANITY

in an informal setting a popular retreat master responds to catholics' deepest concerns

Isaias Powers, C.P.

Nihil Obstat
   Rev. Lawrence Landini, O.F.M.
   Rev. John J. Jennings

Imprimi Potest
   Rev. Andrew Fox, O.F.M.
   Provincial

Imprimatur:
   +Daniel E. Pilarczyk, V.G.
   Archdiocese of Cincinnati
   September 29, 1977

The *Nihil Obstat* and *Imprimatur* are a declaration that
a book or pamphlet is considered to be free from doctri-
nal or moral error. It is not implied that those who have
granted the *Nihil Obstat* and *Imprimatur* agree with the
contents, opinions or statements expressed.

Illustrations by Kieran Quinn
Cover photo by Michael Reynolds

SBN 0-912228-48-2

CONTENTS

A NOTE ABOUT THE
CHOICE OF THE TITLE

This is not so much an introduction as a request. I ask you to invite me past your living room into your kitchen, where we can be friends informally.

Only by your invitation can I get past the fancy teacups and the tiny cookies and the "accepted polite talk" of the parlor . . . and move into the straight-back chair, loosen my clerical collar, drink coffee from one of your plain old mugs and talk about the things that are really on your mind.

You know how it is with friends. You have two kinds. One kind is what I would call "parlor friends." They get as far as the living room—the "best room"—reserved for formal occasions. The children (indeed, the whole family) must be on their best behavior, because "company has come." You are affable and polite. You watch what you say and what you do. You keep the conversation on safe subjects. You drink coffee or tea from the best china and balance cleverly-designed cookies on your napkined knee. You are guarded in approach—anxious, above all, to please the guest. Then, after an hour or so, you shake hands and say, "It was a lovely visit; you must come and visit us again."

And that's that.

Then there is another kind—your *real* friends. Somehow, friends who fit this category either start out or end up around the kitchen table. You don't have to "mind your manners" or worry about how to express yourself. You can grope for words as you wrestle with real problems; you know they will grope with you. You can blurt out your own way of explaining just what it was that made you happy yesterday; you know that your friend can hear the beating of your heart and will not just listen to your halting words.

You can put on your old slippers, roll up your sleeves, take off the stiff coat, drink out of the every-day cups, share a sandwich from a paper plate. You don't have to worry about being embarrassed or misunderstood. You can feel at home and talk about things that are personally important.

This is what I want to do. If you will invite me to sit around the "kitchen table" of your imagination, I'll be able to relax, listen to what you have often "wanted to ask a priest if only they weren't so busy," and respond the way I do when I talk with friends with whom I feel at home.

There is one drawback to this book, of course. I've never actually been in your home. I don't know you personally. So your kitchen—and our coffee break—has to be worked on by my imagination, too.

I have, however, met many people like you. In the course of years, giving hundreds of retreats, I've had many opportunities to listen and respond to people in a "let-the-hair-down, roll-up-the-sleeves, let's-be-ourselves" setting that I call *kitchen-table conversations*. Every one of the subjects of this book has come from such a setting. Someone on retreat (man, woman, nun, college or high school student, new acquaintance or old friend) would trust me. We would talk in my office or while walking around the monastery garden or while actually sitting around a kitchen table. Heart-felt problems would come up—personal questions that called for further understanding or appreciative encouragement. They were not looking for lecture-hall intellectualism or pulpit oratory or "living-room" cliches. They were looking for a friend who would listen and respond to the words and the feelings of what they said.

This book has taken a long time. The 20 essays are "remembered conversations" that have come up often in the last 15 years. I can still recall the incident which moved me to put these conversations into writing. Three men were talking to me, late Saturday night, on a weekend retreat. We were in the lounge, relaxed, drinking coffee from plastic cups. All three had the same problem (I've heard it many times before and since): "How can I get my youngster to go to Mass? He refuses to go because he says, 'Why go if I'm not getting anything out of it?' "

I replied, "Well, what reasons do you give?" They admitted they said: 1)"Because I'm telling you to!"; or 2) "Because it's a sin if you don't!" Then I

3

said, "These reasons are true enough; but they are not very good motivating answers. There are many other ways to explain why it's good to go to Mass, even though one is not 'getting anything out of it.' " They said, "Okay, name a few." They put me on the spot.

Then I started thinking and talking at the same time. Words and ideas just came to me. Ideas did not come out of nowhere, of course. I had wrestled with the problem of churchgoing before. Many thoughts—coming from Scripture and common sense, Aristotle and modern psychology—had been weaving in and out at the back of my mind. But new connections did come to me—new ways of putting together insights from the wide range of concepts given me by prayer and books and people of my past. These new connections helped me to put a different twist to old truths I had already come to live by. It was as if the Holy Spirit caught the mood of the moment and clicked things into place. I am more conscious of having "backed in" to these ideas than of logically working them out ahead of time.

So I did my best, on that occasion, to name a few more reasons for going to Mass. What developed was essentially what is written in Chapter 18. It seemed to help the three men on retreat. So I thought it might help others the same way.

All the essays have resulted from similar dialogues "around the kitchen table." They are ideas that have occurred to me—at the moment—in response to concerns other people have brought up. I have tried to remember some of the typical ways in which friends have expressed these concerns and feelings to me. (This is why so many "quotations" are sprinkled throughout the book.) Then I have tried to remember the words I said and the way I said them.

Each of these essays can be read during a coffee break or while waiting for your husband to get home, or your wife to get ready to go out or while beginning to get drowsy enough to fall asleep. I'd like to think of the book in such surroundings—with your hair let down and your real self thinking.

Finally, my deepest reason for writing this book is to help you invite Jesus from the "parlor" to the "kitchen table" of your heart. Doubtless, you are at least a "living-room friend" of his. (You never would have picked up this book if our Lord were not on some kind of speaking terms with you.) But only you have the power to invite Jesus into the place of more intimate love, mutual esteem and friendship.

If I can help this to happen, in any small way, then the book was worth it—and I am glad I wrote it.

GOD: LIFE OF THE PARTY
OR SPOILSPORT?

Which Version Are We To Believe?

God has received a "bad press" through the centuries, even though he went to a lot of trouble trying to make sure it would be otherwise. He sent his own Son—his own "press agent"—who constantly talked of his Father in terms of joy and having a party with guests who are supposed to enjoy themselves immensely. That's what Jesus says about God. Since he's the only Son, he ought to know.

But we have decided differently. God—in our version—is a killjoy, a spoilsport, an anxious worrier, powerfully disapproving of our imperfections.

Jesus says one thing. We, so often, feel another. What goes on here, anyway? Why is our version so different from his?

It is as though we gather together all the bad feelings about ourselves, make a movie out of them, put them up on a big wide screen in the back of our brains, play it over and over to ourselves (even though it makes us feel miserable), and then assume that God is the producer/director of the dismal melodrama. Then we complain that God must be a terrible God to make such a bad movie about us and make us feel so unhappy while we watch it.

Perhaps there is something of the primitive child deep in all adults, a child that cannot escape from "magical thinking." Magical thinking is the way children have of coping with early reality. They are afraid of things too powerful for them; they are ashamed of some of the things they do. They cannot live with all this fear and blame, so they call to service their vivid imagination and make terror and guilt an outward thing. It gets "distanced." It is pretended to be not a part of them. It resides in a giant "bad guy"—an ogre, a monster or a "god." Often, this early sense of "the powerful other" stays with them all their lives.

Then, as if this were not bad enough, they may also have experienced an early religious training that turned God into a "spoiler." Some important people in their lives used God as one would use the police force—to keep everybody in line and law-abiding.

It is something like the sad histories of so many dope addicts after World War II. Take the case of Jim. After being wounded up front, he was hospitalized in a makeshift barracks. The orderly was overtired and overworked. "For God's sake," he thought to himself (but he really meant "for *my* sake"), "I've got to get some rest. I can't listen to Jim and the others crying in their pain!" He gave Jim dope, and did so regularly, so he could get eight hours of uncluttered snooze. Then Jim was hooked, and hurt, with a hunger for chemical peace all the rest of his unhappy life.

Something like this goes on with God. So many people get hooked on the idea about God in the same way. Parents, baby-sitters, older brothers and sisters, teachers want to get some rest from the hyperactive "whys" and whines of a child. They also want to strengthen their moral authority with the imperatives of a powerful deity who is obviously on their side.

Perhaps they have said, in the same mood of impatience manifested by the orderly:

"You hit your baby brother—God will punish you for that."

"I'll tell your father how naughty you've been, and then you'll get it."

"You know how obedient the little boy Jesus was to this parents. How sad you make him because you are not obedient to us."

"You fibbed! You'd better tell that in confession."

"Remember, angels watch you always and they cry if you look at that part of your body."

Things like that.

So God, and all God's representatives, become a repository of power and something to fear. There are so few ways to please God and so many ways to disappoint him. Little by little, it becomes an impossible task.

Jesus comes into our world with talk about his Father being exuberantly happy, the source of tremendous vitality, having life to give us to the full. This Father, apparently, wants to have a party all the time with friends he really likes to be with. Yet all the while, our child-trained feelings react negatively: "Who wants to go to a party where the host is always ready to weep for my faults or sigh with disappointment? Who needs a God who will send me to a house of correction where I will shape up or be nagged about my mistakes?"

Now, please, pause a moment, enjoy your coffee—and let me have some—and let's both shift positions. If the body shifts, it will be a little easier to shift the mind as well. I'm asking you to change your fear-ridden and guilt-trapped ideas about God the Father. I'm asking you to cut away from those opinions given you by mistaken adults. I'm asking you to empty your head of all preconceptions and let Jesus tell you straight about his Father—not what *you* think his Father is, but what *he* thinks he is. And

Jesus is the only one who knows.

It is a large order to "shift gears" in theology—to understand God as our celebrating Father instead of a critical baby-sitter who wants to get some rest. Perhaps it would be easier to make the shift through Jesus. With him we have celebration at its best.

Not only did our Lord talk about his Father in terms of joy and a festive party. He also practiced what he preached. On one occasion he positively thrilled with joy. The disciples (Lk 10:17-21) were having a happy reunion. (One gets the impression it was very much like the locker room—champagne and all—of a baseball team that just won the World Series.) The 72 had just come back from their first road trip. They were successful. They had achieved. They had healed. The words they had spoken were well-received. Their God-given power to restore life was stronger than the devil's power to lead people into death and discouragement. It was a great feeling. They shared their enthusiasm and mission stories with the Lord and with each other.

At this point, St. Luke mentions that Jesus "thrilled with joy." He celebrated the occasion with them. He praised them: "That's wonderful. I rejoice with you. And remember this—you are great, and my Father loves you, not only for the good that you did, but also, and even more so, for the fact that you are my friends. Your names are written in the book of life."

At this point, St. Luke mentions that Jesus "rejoiced in the Holy Spirit and said: 'I offer you praise, O Father, Lord of heaven and earth, because what you have hidden from the learned and the clever you have revealed to the merest children. Yes, Father, you have graciously willed it so' " (Lk 10: 21-22).

Then Jesus prayed. He was so filled with joy, he couldn't stop. We can imagine him saying, "Thanks to the joy of my disciples, I thank you, Father, for the wonderful love and life you've given to mankind. On the occasion of our celebration, I now have even more reason to praise you for your goodness."

Isn't this a lovely idea? We can think of all the normal times that give us reason to celebrate: a child getting a good report card, a wedding, a woman giving birth, a priest being ordained, someone being promoted or praised, a person being loved, a home team winning the championship. These, and a thousand more, are all ways of coming together with friends and saying, "Good! We're pretty good, aren't we?" And when this happens, it still provides the occasion for Jesus to rejoice.

Life has been celebrated. Love and gratitude and care have been proclaimed. Jesus ratifies our natural loyalties and tells us again that we are worthwhile, and should continue to celebrate. But he gives the deepest reason: "Nevertheless, do not rejoice so much in the fact that devils are subject to you as that your names are inscribed in heaven" (Lk 10:20).

Jesus could add that, thanks to our joy, he has even more reason to be grateful and to praise his Father for the wonderful ways he gives wisdom and love to little ones.

This way of thinking about God is a far cry from thinking of him as a cranky critic who can't be pleased by anything. It is a better way to begin.

We start with our own joy. This develops in us a sense of accomplishment, a feeling of self-worth. We share these with our Lord, as his first friends did.

Then Jesus is further stimulated to increase his joy—
to praise our friendship and to thank his Father.
Finally, we are able to relish-by-anticipation the
great party in heaven, where temporary joys will be
furthered to unimaginable limitlessness.

It seems to be a good way to begin this book of
essays, too.

THE MESSAGE IS BREAD, NOT STONES

Jesus, the Radical Revolutionary

I once heard of a psychiatrist who had a way of understanding his patients even before the first interview. While the perspective clients were in the waiting room, he'd ask them to write down their ideas on: "Who is Jesus Christ? What did he say and do? What does he mean to you?"

The doctor claimed that the responses didn't give him any new insights about Jesus but they did give him insights about the respondents. One would remember our Lord's anger. He would see Christ making whips and throwing the moneylenders (dirty capitalists!) out of the Temple; he would hear Christ castigating the power structure of the Pharisees (the decadent "in group"). Another would, with wistful despair, remember how differently Jesus approached the sinners of his time; gently and without raised voice he would (according to this interpretation) "forgive everybody everything. He would let people 'just be' as they went their way to wherever or whatever they wanted."

Most people, it seems, like to think of Jesus as a kind of "divine sanction," or support, of the peculiar turn of personality that they already have. "I am like this—and it's okay to be so because so is Jesus." (Which means: "I am an angry revolutionary; so is Jesus;" or "I am too lazy to change my compulsions; I just want to be for-given-in-to. So why can't people do for me what Jesus did?")

This tendency to treat Christ with our own pre-packaged selective bias is a very difficult tendency to overcome. There are two dangers involved. The first is one that could be called the "puppy dog syndrome"—turning God into reverse: a harnessed pet that is broken in to our personal needs. We are the lord and master; God is the dog. There are no contradictions or challenges; does a dog challenge his master? A dog simply obeys and applauds the biases of behavior that already exist, wagging his head or his tail like some benign Buddha.

But Jesus is a radical revolutionary in the more powerful sense. He is the Lord and Master. He will not live in our hearts unless he is permitted to turn topsy-turvy all our thinking, attitudes and behavior. He will change us, taking the initiative in our lives. We will not change him or dress him up in our likeness as though he were an uncomplaining, doll-like prince of peace. Our role is to listen, not to dictate. Our responsibility is to embrace everything he tells us, not to simplify his revelation by quoting passages acceptable to us and throwing out the uncomfortable ones.

Hence, if our temperament is one that gets angry quickly, the indignation of Jesus should not be so well remembered as his gentleness and his patient love. On the other hand, if our personality is one that gets lazy quickly or is afraid to act for fear of being criticized by worldly people, it would be well to ponder on his indignation and to remember the uncompromising challenges he puts to us.

If we don't let Jesus give balance to our lives—*his* way—we are treating him like a puppy dog, subservient to us. But the "puppy dog syndrome" is only one extreme. There is another one, even more dangerous. While the first tends to make God loose and pliable, the second tends to make him stern and inflexible. This one is directed toward God the Father instead of his incarnate Son.

It could be called the "corporation meany syndrome." It is "corporation" in the sense that it incorporates all the people who have treated us meanly from the time of our birth. The psychological dynamic goes like this:

> "Mom neglected me when she kept talking on the telephone instead of paying attention to me."
>
> "Dad disapproved of me when I didn't get straight A's in school."
>
> "My older brother and sister were often too busy with their own affairs to bother with me."
>
> "My family ignored my enthusiasms and belittled my self-doubts."
>
> "My friends at school often razzed me (too

short/too fat/long nose/pug nose/big ears/four eyes/acne/accent). And they also warned me that I'd be 'out of it' unless I acted just like the rest of them."

"So much of my life was threatened with 'You'd better behave, or else you'll get it!'"

And so it goes. New mean characters enter the story as the person ages: the boss, the neighbors, fellow workers, playground bullies, village gossips, pastors, bureaucrats, doctors, orderlies, etc.

Then God comes on the scene. The usual routine is to put him "out there" with the others—Mom at her most uncaring times, Dad at his most disapproving, family at their most preoccupied, friends at their most threatening. Out of all this mix of unhappy memories, God gets lumped together as "The Great Disapproving, Rejecting, Belittling *Meany*" who is either 1) too busy to be bothered with me, or 2) full of imperious threats, warning me, "You'd better behave, or else you'll get it!" ("It," in this case, means the most frightening weapons in the arsenal of fear—bad luck, ill health, death and the doom of hell.)

Many people, to a greater or lesser extent, think of God this way. They first of all relive how all the "big people" in their past have hurt them, rejected them, or—worst of all—ignored them, leaving them feeling only marginally meaningful. Then they plunk God into this reawakened past and blow him up until he becomes some kind of mysterious "corporate other"—as bad as all the others at their worst.

Now we come to Jesus and his topsy-turvy revelation of the Father. This is where his true genius as a radical revolutionary shines forth. He tells us to change radically, to make a 180-degree shift in our thinking. We are not to base our ideas on what the Father is like by what we have seen of vindictive people (even fathers and mothers) around us. Jesus is the only Son the Father has, and it is *he* who tells us who the Father is.

To understand the Father, we must wash out of our hearts all the hurts that are still there, as a result of other people's meanness and our own. We must fill our hearts with good thoughts, good memories of ourselves. We ought to focus our thoughts on those times when we were at our best, listening to someone with an understanding heart, helping a friend with advice or money, being faithful to a loved one who was trying to pull through sickness or depression, giving life to the party, forgiveness to those who hurt us, strength to the weak, hope to the doubting.

We can image Jesus saying:

"You know how imperfect you are, also. You are not good listeners, or strong, or helpful, all the time. But sometimes you are. And when you, imperfect as you are, do live at your best and love at your very best—*this* is the clue to the right understanding of my Father.

"Maybe your own parents (teachers, bosses) did not seem to care about you, lost in their own preoccupations. My Father is not like that. My Father is like you when you do care about your loved ones—only he is even better than you at your best.

"Maybe some friend has never forgiven you. My Father is not like that. He is like you when you forgave those who did you wrong—only he is better and quicker at forgiving than you ever were.

"Maybe you were made to feel small and left out

by others, and maybe this is why you have such beautiful compassion for those who are down-and-out. My Father is not like those who hurt your feelings. He is like you at your most compassionate moments—only he is even more so.

"The clue to understanding is here. It is my revolution. I've said it before. I've repeated it for almost 2000 years now. Both Matthew and Luke recorded it in my gospel. The figures of speech are not too difficult to grasp. I said, and say it still:

'If a little one asks you for bread,
will you give him a stone?
Or if he asks for a fish,
will you give him a scorpion?

'Therefore if you, imperfect as you are,
know how to give good gifts to your little ones,
how much more
will your Father give good things
to those who ask him."
(cf. Mt 7:7-11; Lk 11:11-13)

"Please, therefore, don't use those hurts (the 'stones') which you have received from others as the way of understanding who my Father is. Use the good memories of yourself—the times you've given the 'bread' of kindness and patient care to others—as the lens by which you see how God is kind to you."

In a way, this essay deals with prayer. It talks about the right attitude to have in our relationship with God. It approaches the subject negatively, suggesting two important attitudes *not* to have. God will do the rest. The Father will send his Spirit to grow us into the love and joy experienced by Jesus—as long as we don't "me-first" him.

As long as we 1) let Jesus be the revolutionary he came to earth to be, not trying to simplify his message to suit our needs, nor fashioning his personality according to the pattern of our preconceptions; and 2) as long as we think of the Father in terms of *us at our best,* not *others at their worst,* then we will have the strong gentleness of Jesus, and be able to be called a Christian after his own heart.

We will love our Father much more confidently too. We'll learn to be grateful for the bread he gives us and be alert for more and more opportunities to give bread to others, so that we can understand God's kindness even better than before.

BE PERFECT — THE WAY GOD GIVES US SUN AND RAIN

Christ's Teaching *Against* Perfectionism

I have only three ideas. They all come from the words of Jesus Christ. The first has already been mentioned: right relationship with God must come from the living goodness remembered in ourselves. To the degree that we acknowledge our gifts of "bread, not stones" to others, we understand how God is the giver of "bread, not stones" to us. The third idea, "The reign of God is already in your midst" (Lk 17:21), will be developed later in this book.

Here I want to begin the middle one, the operational base for the bulk of this book. It is a "behavior saying" of our Lord. It is a paradoxical saying, too. That's not our Lord's fault; his words are not obtuse. He couldn't be any more clear. Yet these words, more than others, have been pulled out of his context—where they were meant to give encouragement—and placed in a man-made torture chamber where they have become weapons of dread, discouragement and scrupulosity.

The behavior saying is, "Be perfect!" That is the way Christ worded his command. And he added (and it does sound frightfully demanding) " . . . *as* your heavenly Father is perfect."

That's it. Black and white. Right there in the Sermon on the Mount. "Be made perfect as your heavenly Father is perfect" (Mt 5:48). Then a certain self-destructive instinct in us says, "I know what Jesus means by this, and I don't like it!"

Interpretations take a number of turns. The favorite one is: "Jesus warns me to be perfect. I am not perfect. 'Everybody' tells me so. I know it for a fact myself. Therefore, I am worthless.

"Didn't 'everybody' tell me (speaking with all the self-assured authority of God) that, 'If a thing is worth doing, it's worth doing perfectly'? I haven't done anything perfectly. At no time could I have said that a day could not have been better, a deed could not have been improved, a motive could not have been nobler, a thought could not have been more pure, a thing-worth-doing could not have taken more pains, more preparation. I despair, ever, of being perfect. Therefore I despair of God."

Another turn faces outward. A different target, but it's the same attack of perfectionism: "My family (or community, or work group, or team, or spouse, or children, or parents, or church) should be perfect. Christ's words. This, then, is the natural expectation. My family (etc., etc.) is not perfect. Therefore I must treat same with a harsh blend of nagging and dissatisfaction."

This is scrupulosity projected onto others. It is the basis for such typical family dramas as:

> "Dad, Dad, I finally did it—I got a 98 per cent in math this month!" (Response: "What happened to the other two points?")
>
> "My husband snores—how can I live with a man who snores?"
>
> "My wife gets tired sometimes after supper. She never did 30 years ago—what's wrong with her?"
>
> "I thought, when I entered religious life, it was a state of perfection; the convent I live in is still far from it!"
>
> "Some priests still smoke cigarettes, after all the surgeon general has said!"
>
> "I'll take no advice from those two people. They have faults; they don't always practice what they preach! So any good ideas they might have are irrevocably blemished by their imperfections."

And so on and on and on.

Much of the modern demand for this "faultlessness/ discovery of fault/ despair of faulty one" sequence stems from a fascination with machines and a desire to make machines out of people. It is a sickness in society, especially noticeable since the Industrial Revolution. It is true that a machine has to be perfect or it is not good at all. If only one of the thousand facets of the spacecraft does not work, the rocket will not reach the moon. If one gear breaks down in the hydroelectric plant, the whole city falls into darkness. If a scientist forgets one little step, the laboratory experiment is all wrong.

But from all this, it does not follow that the boy is not smart because he got one out of 50 problems wrong, that Babe Ruth is a failure because he struck out so often, that a girl is a "bad girl" because she's done a bad thing.

People are not machines. Imperfections of the two classes of creation demand an entirely different kind of handling. If the battery of a car goes bad, the car is bad. It doesn't work. So the mechanic files down the rust on the battery (a kind of "automotive nagging"), concentrating on what's wrong; then the car is ready to roll.

But people can't be fixed by nagging and concentrating on the faulty area. And we can't junk people as we do old cars, leaving them in some abandoned heap to rust, while we go out and get another model. This what often happens, though—either constant nagging about what is wrong or junking the person altogether. The strange thing is that many people who behave this way use Jesus as their authority: "Didn't our Lord command us to be perfect?"

Yes, he did. However, when Jesus told us this, he had a particular thing in mind. The call to be perfect was put at the end of a long series of instructions. Consequently, the meaning Jesus gives this word *perfect* was flavored and explained by all that went before it, and especially by two extremely important symbols—sun and rain—which makes our Lord's way of saying "Be perfect" something completely contrary to our modern perfectionism.

The fullest version of Christ's "explanation" is in St. Matthew (5: 43-48). One can tell, by the way

Jesus warms up to the subject, that a case is not being built up advocating behavior that would nag other people or lead one's self to despair: "You have heard the commandment, 'You shall love your countryman but hate your enemy.' My command to you is: love your enemies, pray for your persecutors" (Mt 5: 43-44).

Another version is: "Love those who tell lies about you." Obviously, Jesus is talking about long-suffering and forgiveness and patience. How, then, can this passage be the excuse for so much short-tempered *short-suffering* of other people's faults and such impatience with our own?

Then the two beautiful metaphors appear. Jesus continues:"This will prove that you are sons of your heavenly Father, for his sun rises on the bad and the good, he rains on the just and the unjust" (Mt 5: 45).

The sun and the rain! These are the two necessary conditions of all life. Without them, we have no grass, no seed, no trees, no shade, no flowers, no eggs, no lambchops, no water, no wood, no sunsets, no rainbows—no life at all.

God the Father is thorough with his gifts, with these two gifts in particular. All share and share alike. He does not let anyone die on the vine or dry up for lack of the bare essentials. He is not snobbish or punishing or impatient. He does not say, "You farmers are lazy; therefore no more sun and rain on your acres! I'm reserving my love only for the good guys." He does not say, "Stay hungry and thirsty, you dishonest people down there; I'm cutting you off from the sources of supply! Without sun and rain nothing will grow and then you'll be sorry for all your faults (nyaah, nyahh)!" God does not act this way. Jesus, his Son, told us so.

Then our Lord continues, in a familiar home-spun style, not without humor, "If you love those who love you, what merit is there in that? Do not tax collectors do as much? And if you greet your brothers only, what is so praiseworthy about that? Do not pagans do as much?" (Mt 5: 46-48).

With all his easy manner of reasoning, Jesus' message is serious and dramatic. We must be exceptional in this matter of "giving sun and rain" to others and to ourselves. It is an extremely difficult response-ability; but we must live up to it if we want to be followers of Christ.

Then comes the bombshell—our Lord's concluding remark, "In a word, you must be made perfect as your heavenly Father is perfect."

St. Luke (6:36) quotes Jesus as saying, in the very same context, "Be compassionate as your Father is compassionate." Both evangelists mean the same.

This teaching is the opposite of perfectionism. If I get down on others because they talk behind my back, or if I nag them for their blemishes of character, or if I mope because they are ungrateful for the good I do them; if I do any of these things, I am effectively withholding the necessities of life from them—refusing to give them "sun and rain," without which there is no growth.

And if I let depression get its hold on me and wallow in self-pity because of my own imperfections, I'm acting contrary to the Father's way of working things out with me.

God patiently sends sunshine and gentle rain to get us to grow again. Often we don't let it happen.

We close the shutters to the sun and stifle ourselves in self-afflicted drought. Sure, we love ourselves when we've had a good day, or have done a good job, or have seen all things run smoothly. But, to paraphrase our Lord, "So what! That's not exceptional. Even pagans do that much. You become a real Christian when you are patient with yourself, even on bad days—when faults are obvious and tears are imminent and life is dreary. That is when the test case comes!

"You must be thorough as my Father is thorough. You must not withhold—from self or from others—the sun of gentleness and the soft rain of patient kindness. Even though the world is blemished (as you are, too), you must continue to give, *un*conditionally, all those things (symbolized by sun and rain) which are needed for the God-given growth of others—and your God-*giving* growth."

HASSLING AND HEALING

Proper Therapy for the Aching Heart

The "sun and rain" style of unconditional love is God's way of healing. We ought to follow his method, instead of using a "darkness and drought" approach.

Take a case in point. Say that a boy just got a new bike. In his fresh enthusiasm he sped too fast around a curve, fell and broke his arm. Now, it would be ridiculous for this eight-year-old to do nothing but moan, shake the arm and wince each time he touched the elbow: "Ouch, it hurts. See? Whenever I put pressure on it—Ooo, how miserable I am!" True enough. But this is not helping the arm.

It would be just as ridiculous for the parents of the boy to keep analyzing the problem: "I know why your arm hurts. It hurts because you broke it. You broke it because you fell off the bike. You fell off the bike because you weren't careful. You weren't careful because you didn't listen to me. You never do. If I told you once, I told you a thousand times (nag, nag, nag)."

This is, no doubt, an accurate estimate of the situation. But it is not helping the boy's arm. Nor is it helping his growth.

What do good parents do? They take him to a doctor. The doctor does not do the healing—not directly. The doctor simply knows how to give the arm rest. He puts it in a cast. It is from the *inside* that healing takes place. The bones, once rested, mend themselves. Then the muscles, little by little, build up again. And after a while, the arm is as good as new.

When the pain is altogether inside us, we can behave unwisely. It is a hurt in the heart that I speak of now. What happens when someone betrays us, rejects us, denies our love or friendship, refuses to follow our advice? What happens, also, when we betray ourselves, deny the best part of us because of our own sin, inefficiency or even clumsiness?

What happens? We do precisely that which is best calculated to keep healing from taking place. Instead of putting the hurts of our heart "in a cast" and letting the scars mend themselves, we irritate the sore and keep checking on ourselves to see if it's still there.

We keep analysing the situation and make an airtight case for ourselves as though we were some highly paid prosecuting attorney. We could even give the case a name, as we brood over incident after incident—we could call it "My Justification for

Being Hurt." Once the case is prepared, we play the role to the hilt and turn friends and acquaintances into a mock jury who must listen—over and over and over again—to the case of "self against that member of my family," or "self against the boss."

But we never say, at the end of our list of grievances, "Case rests!"—for the case never seems to be able to rest.

We heal a broken heart the way we heal a broken arm—give it rest, leave it alone, let the power (which comes from the *inside)* mend the nagging pain.

This is difficult to do. The world, invaded by what I call *comparison ethics,* goes against the proper therapy of a hurt heart. Comparison ethics is in the air we breathe. It can be identified by sentences beginning with: "Why aren't you as good as . . ."

The comic strip "Peanuts" had an interesting example of it. Crabby Lucy is dictating terms to the defenseless dog Snoopy (who is really "everyperson"). She begins, "Charlie Brown has asked me to take care of feeding you today." Then she moves in for her bid for control: "You know what this means, don't you? It means I have you in my *power!* I've had enough of your insults. You'd better behave today, because I control the supper dish. I've got you where I want you!" She concludes with a rather philosophical remark: "The hand that controls the supper dish rules the world!"

This is the most graphic presentation of manipulation that I have ever read. "Controlling the supper dish" is diabolical and efficient. It is used because it *works*—to get others to behave our way. Even little children learn to use it. I remember, when I was a little boy, saying, "Why, Mom? Why

33

can't I stay up to listen to Fibber Magee and Mollie? Joe Wilber's mother lets *him* stay up, and Carl Peglow's and Fred Fleishman's and all the other guys', . . . "

See what I was doing? Implied in my nagging was the statement: "Unless you let me do what I want, I'm going to make you feel that you are not as good a mother as Joe Wilber's or the others!" Sometimes I got my way. It was the most efficient manipulation tool I had. Some instinct in me told me that nobody wants to feel "not as good as" someone else.

Parents use it on children, too:

"Why can't you get as good grades as your older sister?"

"Why can't you make the first team? Your friend did and he doesn't have the natural talent you do!"

"Why can't you be in on time? You cause us much more worry than all your brothers did!"

"Why aren't you as obedient to us as so-and-so is to his parents?

Teenagers use it, too: "Why can't I stay out until two? Everybody else does!" Parents respond with, "I don't care about everybody else. You are not 'everybody else'!" Then the children reply, "Then why do I get 'everybody else' thrown up at me when you want me to be as neat as so-and-so, or as practical, or as brainy, or as popular?"

It's a vicious circle. Spouse to spouse applies the same system of "manipulation by comparison":

"Why can't you make more money or take me out more often? Your brother treats his wife better than you treat me!"

"Why can't you balance the books the way your
   neighbor Sally does?"

"Sure I'm going out again. None of my friends'
   wives nag their husbands about it!"

And so it goes. To understand why this system is
so efficient, go back to the poor dog being threatened
with the empty supper dish. Consider the dog as
everybody and consider the supper dish as un-
satisfied needs. Take these needs out of the physical
into the psychological. What are they? They are the
needs to live a life that is both meaningful and productive. They are the hunger we have to be good for
others—to feel, deep down, that "I'm okay. I'm
somebody, and appreciated as such. In my own
right, I am good as a child, a parent, a spouse, a
fellow worker, a neighbor, a friend. The people significant to me are happy that I am who I am. I make
their world better by my presence."

Everyone has these huge appetites. They could be
summed up in the most basic need of all—the need
to feel worthwhile. This being so, all others are able
to threaten us with comparison ethics by using "supper dish control". We are in their power, if they want
to use this power. We are very likely to flinch if they
say: "You'd better behave according to my dictates,
or I won't feed you with that acceptance you are hungry for—and you will go to bed without your supper!
For I can make you feel *un*worthwhile by comparing
you unfavorably to somebody else. You'll be miserable; and, that way, I'll get you to give in!"

After so many years of such a starvation diet, it
becomes almost second nature to keep irritating ourselves with "unworthwhileness." We begin to do it to
ourselves: "I'm not as good (or as smart, or as pretty,

or as successful, or as happy, or as healthy) as the others."

Then, because we've gone so long without nourishment, it gets to be difficult to take in any solid food. When we are praised or productive or promoted or appreciated, these touches of worthwhileness go unheeded. We just cannot believe we're of any good at all.

It is no wonder, then, that only with great difficulty do we let ourselves be healed from the hurts of the heart. The fact is, of course, that we must—if we want to be Christian. Jesus commanded us to be like his Father in the matter of letting sun and rain help the growth of life and heal the dried-up spirit. Comparison ethics goes against—directly against—this injunction.

Of all the practical plans for self-improvement—and for healing the hassled nerves of others—this is, perhaps, the most practical of all: "It is wrong and sinful for me to nag others by comparing them unfavorably to someone else. Even though it's the quickest way of punishing them and the most efficient way of getting what I want from them, I won't do it.

"And I won't nag myself anymore, either. That's not the way to be healed of my hurts. It won't help to keep irritating the wounds or 'wishing I were as good as ___.' I'll give myself, and others, rest. I'll let the mending come from the inside—with the sun and rain, the love and peace, that are available to me now from God in his gracious presence and from the worthy—and 'worthwhiling'—friends I have."

BETWEEN THE "SHOUT DOWN" AND THE "SHUT OUT"

How to Forgive Without Being Phony

Jesus tells us to be "thorough" or "whole" in our love for self and others, even when it hurts. "Be like my Father (merciful, non-withholding) who causes sun and rain to support the life of everyone—good and bad alike."

Even when it hurts! It hurts to obey our Lord's command when somebody has hurt us. Whenever this happens (I mean an important blow to our self-respect, an insult that devastates or demoralizes) we want to follow either of two counselors that lodge inside our brain and tempt us to be angry.

One counselor tempts us to "shout them down"; the other tempts us to "shut them out." They both give bad advice.

The first one—call him the "blusterer"—see injustice done and wants to square things with an over-dose of retaliation. "Don't let them get away with it" is the motto. "Get even, at all cost" is the strategy.

When Jesus gets remembered for saying, "If someone strikes you on one cheek, give him your other cheek as well," the angry blusterer inside us simply declares this to be impossible.

But the angry blusterer is not a good interpreter of Jesus' words. A better way to understand is to let these words take their meaning from other ways that Jesus acted and other statements that Jesus made (including the one: "Be thorough as my Father's gift of sun and rain").

Remember Good Friday morning. When Jesus was struck on the face by a soldier of the high priest Caiphas, he did not meekly turn his other cheek. He protested, "If I have said anything wrong, produce the evidence, but if I spoke the truth, why hit me?" (Jn 18:23).

Our Lord did not succumb to either extreme. He would not retaliate blow for blow, lowering himself to the soldier's level. But neither did he say, "Yes, you are right. I deserve your blows because I am no good." Jesus stayed his ground; but he gave the man a chance to defend his action. Our Lord did not close off communication.

Jesus was speaking dramatically when he told us to turn the other cheek. A less emphatic expression of at least part of his idea might be worded this way: "Don't close off a person because of his original insult. Give him a chance to explain the meaning of his outburst. Perhaps he didn't mean it as you took it. Perhaps he had a bad day. Perhaps he will change. You know that you say and do insulting things sometimes—on the spur of the moment—that you regret soon afterwards. You don't like it when the person you hurt takes the outburst as your final statement, as though you had only a bad side to your personality and no good side. Well, treat other people the way you want them to treat you."

St. Luke records not only Christ's words, but also the meaning that he gives these words. In Chapter six, verse 29, Jesus tells us to "turn the other cheek." In the following two verses, he explains what he means in another way: "Do to others what you would have them to do to you." Here, as with many other statements that Jesus made, it is important to: 1) understand the context, the particular flavor, that our Lord gives to the words he says; 2) understand the "whole person Jesus" saying these words, verifying his teaching with the reality of his lived-out situation. In this case, it is important to read all of Chapter six of St. Luke's Gospel to get the context and to remember that the Jesus who said these words was the same Jesus who did not turn the other cheek when he was before Caiphas and his brutal soldier.

The person Jesus who acted Good Friday morning and who spoke in St. Luke's Chapter six is also the same person who gives a way to love someone "negatively" even when we cannot do so "positively." Once again, the "sun and rain" instruction can be helpful. We must be like God, our Father, who does *not* refuse to give the conditions for life and growth. God does not rate the wicked equal to the good. But he nevertheless continues to love even those who reject him. God never punishes the wicked in such a way as to cut them off from any chance to change. His unconditional gift of sun and rain guarantee their survival and continuance as well.

We can do this much—indeed, we *must*—even when the smart of an offense still stings. The act of forgiving is not quite so difficult when we think negatively *(not* refusing love) instead of positively (actually embracing the offender). More often than not, it is emotionally impossible to go up to someone who has just offended us—hurt us deeply—and give this person a big smile or start a friendly conversation as if nothing happened. We just can't do it. Anyhow, the offender would more than likely mistrust our sudden effusiveness.

I don't see how Jesus can expect the impossible. Perhaps we are not expected to "turn the other cheek" in a positive, "Hail-fellow-well-met-let's-forget-whatever-happened" optimism. But Jesus still does demand that we *don't refuse to love* those who hurt us.

So much for the blusterer's bad advice—the one who says, "Shout them down." The other counselor inside our heads is just as bad. This one urges "Shut them out. Treat them as a nobody, as nonexistent! Punish them with silent treatment, worthy only of uncommunicative contempt!"

Yet, even though the style of the two is different, they both deal with a hurt in unproductive ways. They both make matters worse for the offended person as well as for the offender.

Observe the decision we must make in this typical challenge: We see a person who has insulted us come up the side of the street we're walking on. We have four options. They are:

1. Greet him warmly and shake his hand—

"Hail fellow, well met." (We can't do that; we are still smarting from his hurt.)

2. Stay on the same side of the street and punch him in the nose or give him verbal abuse so that he will never forget what he did to us. (Of course, this way, he has no choice but to remain our enemy forever.)

3. Put our nose in the air and walk over to the other side of the street. (Treat him as a nobody—refuse him the sun and rain of mercy—abort all chance of reconciliation.)

4. Stay on the same side of the street, simply say hello, mention some innocuous thing like the weather, and suggest that maybe later "We can get together and have a good talk"—that is, keep communication lines open.

This fourth choice is the only Christian one. It is the one we must take when it comes to the black sheep of the family, too. Perhaps the family cannot convincingly embrace the renegade, welcoming him home with open arms. But no family has the right to banish anyone into the limbo of nonentity—punishing forever with "silent treatment." "Not refusing sun and rain" means *not refusing* to write to him; *not judging* him (only God can judge a person's secret heart; *not denying* him remembrances at birthdays and Christmas; *not breaking off* the lines of communication.

It is a consoling thought. Jesus does not ask the impossible. He does demand, though, that we be exceptional in our behavior. Pagans retaliate in kind—blow for blow, insult for insult, deep freeze for deep hurt. Christians must be different. We cannot break

41

down the possibilities for growth or the chances for reconciliation. We cannot refuse "sun and rain" to others.

Dr. Carl Rogers has an excellent and insightful analysis of unproductive, as opposed to helpful, behavior. He calls unproductive behavior "that-which-puts-other-people-on-the-defensive" — that which brings out the worst in others. We would call unproductive behavior *sins*—offenses *and* negligences against our neighbor.

There are four principal ways by which we "bring out the worst" in other people:

1. by judging them;
2. by trying to manipulate them;
3. by acting superior to them;
4. by treating them as though they didn't exist.

The first method of unproductive behavior is *evaluation;* whenever we judge someone, assess his motives, assume we "know what makes him tick," we trigger defense mechanisms in that person. Description, instead of evaluation, is a better way to communicate. (This will be discussed in the next essay.)

The second method, *control,* has already been discussed in Chapter four. Whenever our main concern is to manipulate others ("Why can't you be as good as . . .?") we can expect them to feel used. Once they feel used, they'll be defensive and act "unproductively" against us.

The third method in this list is called *emphasizing superiority.* Whenever we keep harping on that which makes us better than somebody else—

"I'm older."

"I'm younger."

"I'm the boss."

"I've had more experience."

"I have more schooling."

"I know the ropes."

"I've been sick longer."

"When I was your age, I walked to school and
had it tough and really had to work."

Whenever any kind of superiority is emphasized,
the tendency is to put the other person down, make
him feel inferior, bring out the worst in the one put
down. The sense of equality brings out the best in
others. Constant references to "what makes me better than you" brings on defensive behavior. This,
too, will be taken up in detail later.

The last, and the most deadly, of these behavior
sins is something that is rarely considered when we
make an examination of conscience. Dr. Rogers
even has a clumsy word for it—he calls it *neutrality*
as opposed to *empathy*. Neutrality is what I call the
"silent treatment"—reducing someone to a nobody,
relegating a person to the world of nonentity.

The deadliest sin of all! Yet it is so often excused:
"I didn't *do* anything. I didn't *say* anything." True
enough. You did not throw stones. But you refused
to give bread. You neglected to give the "sun and
rain" without which there is no growth.

What is the most oppresive kind of punishment,
after all? Is it not silent treatment? Isn't it this that
children fear from their parents most? Isn't the
threat of exclusion the most devastating threat
among teenagers or any peer group? Isn't "not
speaking to one another" the last straw in a marriage
break-up?

Neutrality is the opposite of love. To reduce anybody to a "nothing of importance" closes off all

further chance for friendship. There is some way for every other hurt to be healed. There is no way for a nobody to become a somebody again. Humpty Dumpty has crashed on the cold shoulder, and all the king's horses and all the king's men can't put Humpty back together again.

Empathy is different. Empathy is what religion calls charity. It is what our Lord describes as "not refusing the sun and rain to anyone, even though they are dishonest, ungrateful or insulting." Empathy charges us to do for others what we would want them to do for us and keep communication lines open—even though we cannot turn the other cheek as yet. Empathy does not one-sidedly close off the possibility of a change of heart.

Empathy is Jesus Christ who, even though Simon Peter denied him publicly, rose from the dead and stayed on Simon's side of the street and offered him a second chance ("Peace be with you"). He gained a friend whom he could easily have punished by the silent treatment.

Empathy is the sun and the rain making it possible for peace to exist and love to grow in those relationships where there were only hot blusterings and cold silences before.

THE DEADLY 'DOUBLE YOU'

Shoulder Shrugs and Pointed Fingers

There is a story told me by an older priest while we were giving a parish mission. He said that it was his ordinary custom to surprise a certain type of penitent with a twofold penance: "Whenever anyone says in confession, 'Bless me Father, I have sinned. I got angry at my husband because he did this and that to me. I got impatient with the children because they behaved this way and that . . .,' I would say, at the end, 'Well, ma'am, for *your* sins say one Hail Mary, and for your *family's* sins say three rosaries."

The point is simple enough. The lady in the box was not confessing her own sins. She was, in fact, justifying her anger and indignation. It was her husband's sins, and her children's, that she was confessing.

It is the humor of the story I want to emphasize. It is humorous to me because it so very rarely happens. Seldom does anyone go to confession this way. Almost always the mood of communication is personal sorrow and the style of communication is *first person singular*—"*I* have done wrong; *I* am sorry." That is why hearing confessions is such a positive experience.

I've been a priest for 15 years. I've been the instrument of Christ's mercy in this sacrament for somewhere between seven and 30 thousand people. Before I was ordained, I wondered what would happen to me after I started hearing confessions. I am optimistic by nature. I wondered if I would change after listening, hour upon hour, as people admitted to me the seamy side of their lives—their selfishness and cowardice and sins. Would I turn into a pessimist and lose hope in people once I opened myself to all this avalanche of expressed guilt?

As a matter of fact, the very opposite is true. I have been privileged to experience people at their very best—their most honest and sincere. They speak in the first person singular. Considering the difficulty they are up against—temptations to sin, situations which so readily lead to frustration and impatience, so many reasons for despairing—I marvel at the courage and resilience of most people. I thank God for the goodness I see in those who accept forgiveness and new life again.

Everyone has had this good feeling at times. It's usually a one-to-one communication with a trusting friend, perhaps around the kitchen table. The friend will be honest and specific, instead of guarded and vague. The pronoun is the first person, not second person—it is "I," not "you".

Every Saturday night, I have a discussion with retreatants on communication problems. At the outset, I ask each one, "Why did you choose this discussion? What problem area do you have in mind?" My expectation was that the retreatants would talk about themselves and their situations, using statements that began with the pronoun that referred personally to them: "*I* have trouble communicating with my spouse, my workers, my teenage children, my parents because, when I do this or that, I don't seem to be getting through."

The phrases did not come across this way. The phrases went like this:

> "You can't seem to jump the barrier with your kids these days."
>
> "You shudder when you think about what's going on in movies and magazines."
>
> "You try to explain things to your wife, but she won't listen to you."

I try to suggest (sometimes!) that I, personally, don't have trouble jumping the barrier, that I don't shudder, that I have no wife. I also suggest that some wives do listen. Not every married woman in the world can be categorized as a non-listener just because one man has the opinion that one of them seems to be. So why use the vague pronoun "you" and include everybody in one lump, as though misery loves company?

I plead with them to take responsibility for their own feelings: "Instead of '*You* can't seem to jump the barrier with your kids,' say '*I* can't seem to,' say '*I* shudder,' say '*My* wife won't listen,' say '*My* father yells.' "

Then, and only then, can something positive be done about communication. The "you" is deadly because it ends up with a shrug of the shoulders and a fatalistic sigh—it means: "What can *anyone* do?" The "I" suggests challenge and a probe of possibilities—"What can *I* do?"

This is the first way of using the "deadly you" when the word, in all honesty, should be "I." It goes unnoticed most of the time; yet it is deadly because it drains off personal responsibility. As long as the feeling remains—"What can you do?"—the implied message is, "I can't do anything about it because it is everybody's fate!" The *you* intones a defeatist attitude. That's what makes it so deadly.

The second "deadly you" is more obvious. It is the "evaluative you" which Carl Rogers described as that which is bound to bring out defensive and unproductive behavior in other people. Not only Carl Rogers—it is Jesus himself who warns us, over and over, "Do not judge, lest you be judged by my Father."

Evaluating other people's motives, meanings or mistakes is judging. It assumes that I know the inside working of another person's character:

"You hate me!"
"You don't love me anymore!"
"You are deliberately avoiding my question!"
"You are boring!"

What comeback does the person have? Either 1) to admit, "Yes, you are right. I am no good." Or 2) to retaliate by making an evaluative statement right back:

"If you would only change, then I wouldn't hate you so much!"

"It wasn't me who started the cold war. You
did!"

"You always avoid my questions. How do you
like it when somebody else dishes it out to
you?"

"I'm not boring. You're the one who's too
preoccupied to listen!"

And the "Battle of the Pointed Finger" gets
under way. Both sides lose, of course. Nobody wins.
It wasn't meant to be a win/lose game, but it turned
out to be just that.

It is easy to point the finger, to play the game of
"you." No risk is taken. The person called "I" is the
cool cat—disengaged, uninvolved, pointing out what
is wrong with the person called "you." The image is
that of a comfortable and protected television booth,
high above the stands, protected from the noise and
dirt of the football field; the judgmental "finger
pointer" is the cool commentator expressing criti-
cism of the errant players moving around in the
game of life below.

A more honest way of communicating has the
word "I" sprinkled liberally all over. "I feel
unloved"; "I feel avoided"; "I am bored." Then
dialogue can go somewhere. There is a difference
between "I am bored" and "you are boring." It may
be that I am tired at the moment, or preoccupied, or
uninterested in that particular subject. Any of these
has nothing to do with the other individual. Another
likelihood is that perhaps he is boring to me, but not
to others. A number of opportunities are available,
but they would all be closed off by the pointed-
finger statement, "You are boring!"

The "you" approach is safer, though. If I say I am

49

bored, I run the risk of discovering the fault is as much mine as it is his. Then I am no longer safe in the TV booth; I'm down on the playing field myself.

Dr. Rogers tells this story on himself. (It is more difficult to practice this than preach it.) One night, at the end of a party, he and his wife quarrelled. They were angry at each other. The wife was driving, too fast for safety, over a wet, winding road. The husband was afraid of an accident. Ordinarily, he would not tell her this, straight out. Ordinarily, he would have pretended to be the detached observer, cooly pointing out what was wrong with her: "You're angry, aren't you! You don't care whether we skid or not! Typical woman driver—taking your anger out on a poor car!"

Then she would have replied: "You're always criticizing my driving! Didn't you take your anger out on the poor car when you slammed the door?" And another fight would have developed in earnest.

This time he decided to practice what he preached. He decided to describe his feelings, rather than evaluate her behavior. He said, simply, "Honey, I'm scared to go this fast over a slippery road."

It was risky for him to put it this way. He was taking a chance. All she had to do was go faster or stay the same speed. This would be the most effective way of saying, by implication, "I don't care about your feelings. You don't count!" It would have hurt. Actually (though she was still too angry to talk as yet) she did slow down. This made him feel good. He was loved. She cared by responding to his honest description of his feelings.

It is riskier to be personal than to be judgmental. We make ourselves vulnerable to a rebuke, or, worse, the silent rebuff of a shrug that says, "I don't care how you feel." It is difficult to be honest about our feelings and take a chance of being hurt again; but it is the only way love can grow and communication lines can stay open.

Jesus could have "played it cool." Late in the evening of Holy Thursday, he could have said, "I don't need anybody. You men are not really my friends. You don't even care enough to stay with me—even to stay awake. Well, it doesn't matter. I'm tough! I can go it alone!"

Jesus said nothing of the sort. He simply described himself and waited for their response to his need.

They fell asleep in the Garden of Gethsemane. This hurt. It hurt even more because he had already admitted that he needed them. Even so, our Lord stayed true to himself.

Then, after Easter, there was no recrimination, no pointed finger. There was no hint of any judgmental put-downs. He did not say, "You ran away. You left me alone. You are cowards. You can't be trusted, can you?" None of that. It was a gift of forgiveness and a description of his good feelings toward them: "Peace be with you . . . . As the Father has sent me, so I send you" (Jn 20:21). He trusted them to build his Church.

This is lively talk. It radiates the atmosphere of confidence and love. It heals the men already beaten down by their own guilt. The "pointed-finger you" and the vague "you" of fatalism are deadly. They box people into a corner of despair and leave them with no recourse except to come out fighting, usually hitting below the belt.

A Christian is one who lives as Christ would live, as he did live while on earth. A Christian, therefore, is one who radiates "lively talk," keeping open the lines of communication with the sun and rain of mercy, making it possible for forgiveness to have a chance to grow.

An enemy of Christ—an *un*christian—is one who uses the tactic of silent treatment or either one of the deadly "double you's." The sun is shuttered with remembered hurts; the growth-giving rain is refused with a *hummph* and an upturned nose. And nothing happens. The soil is dry. And Jesus has no place to give judger or judged that peace which is his alone to give.

The gift of peace is his. But the choice to let this peace take place is ours. The choice depends on how we use the shrugged shoulder, the pointed finger, the sometimes deadly word, *you.*

HOW TO HANDLE A 'SNOW WHITE EXPERIENCE'

The Danger in Doing Good

Sometimes it is better to make a point obliquely than to say it straight out. It seems to me that this essay is one of those times.

The point I want to make is that emphasis on superiority can make people defensive. When we concentrate on "how good we are," we can bring out the worst in other people—who, by implication, are somehow not so good. There is danger, therefore, lurking in the very goodness of the good deeds we perform.

Obviously, this is a difficult point to make. I don't want to discourage anybody from doing good; yet I do want to serve warning about the danger in doing it. "Do-gooding" can turn a Christian into a Pharisee. Also, if not handled properly, it can make other people defensive and the do-gooder very depressed.

These are hard words. Let me explain myself obliquely, by looking at what happened to Snow White in Walt Disney's popular film version of the fairy tale.

Let me retell the story, because I saw it fresh this year, 37 years after I saw it the first time. Let's see now . . .

Once there was this good, pretty, hard-working, "put-upon" girl (read you and me, of whatever age or sex). She fled from a fearful situation (in her case, home and a wicked stepmother; in our case, it could be almost anything). She was with friends, the seven little men. She was happy enough taking care of the cottage. But she had a dream—that some day her prince would come and change her life into queenly, wifely, perfect happiness (dreams such as we all have, one way or another).

So much for the setting. Now comes the experience with the devil. Two devils in this case—one, an external devil, the jealous witch who hated Snow White; the other, the devil inside Snow White, who loved herself too dearly.

First, the outside devil worked strictly on her own: "Have a nice apple, little girl? See how beautiful it is, how tasty it must be!" These temptations did not work. Snow White was a good person. She could not be tempted straightforwardly.

The animals and birds came to the rescue of their friend. They saw behind the ruse of the old hag, detected evil, and spun the woman round and round until she was dizzy and breathless.

Then Snow White—kindness herself—showed

exemplary compassion. She was a very good person and here was an opportunity to help someone who needed her. She "did her good turn for the day." Forth came the arm to lean on, the chair to sit on, the soup to gain strength by.

Then the witch saw she had Snow White hooked. The outside devil worked on the inside devil: "My pretty thing, you have been so kind to me. You deserve a reward. The reward for being kind is to have control over others. I have this apple. It's a magic apple. Take a bite and make a wish, and your wish has to come true. You will control the destiny—and the timing—of your charming prince. He will be at the beck and call of your magic and you can force him to make you happy. After all, you deserve it—have you not been good to the seven little people and most giving and charitable to me? Take a bite—you deserve to be rewarded."

Well, as you know, she bit (both literally and figuratively). But she was thwarted. Destiny was not in her control. The prince did not show up. She was not rewarded.

So she went into a coma—no longer good for herself or any of her friends. For a long time she was passive, having no opportunity to do good, or earn rewards, or be in control of any giving-receiving relationship.

Then she was ready, finally, for the happy ending. Prince Charming came—on *his* initiative and in *his* good time. He saw her need and loved her well because she needed love. He kissed her. She came to life. She was loved and she loved back. And they still live, every year, happily ever after.

There's a bit of Snow White in us all. Most peo-

55

ple are good people. Good people cannot be tempted, in a straightforward way, to be evil or proud or insensitively selfish. But good people can be tempted when the devil works out of our own goodness.

The setup for the con job is: 1) faithfulness to duty (like Snow White cooking and cleaning the cottage), and 2) generous acts of kindness (like hospitality to the old hag). Then good people sit back and reflect: "I am good, kind, faithful, generous in my giving relationships. It's time *I* should be rewarded. The reward I want is control—magic control over the destiny of others: God to respond to my demands and on my time schedule, dreams for prosperity to come true, friends and family to be so grateful for my goodness to them they will do just what I want."

This was the mismanagement of the Pharisees in the time of Christ. The Pharisees were good people. They were upright, faithful (though to their own traditions), generous (according to their own scales). Their problem was that they harnessed man-made interpretations to the good that they did. They assumed that initiative was theirs in all their actions and even worse, they postured for privilege, based on the good they did, and presumed God's compliance to their demands.

Then Jesus came, preaching a different message: "Man does not take the initiative. God does. God begins the whole process of doing good. Man simply receives this good and humbly does God's will, as a tenant farmer prospering on land that has been undeservedly bestowed."

The phrase, "Glory to God in the highest, and peace to men of goodwill," is dangerously misleading. It implies that man first shows goodwill, performing acts of goodness. Consequently, God has to dole out *shalom* as a reward (like Prince Charming coming down on schedule). No, the phrase goes, "Peace to those on whom *God's* goodwill rests." (It is the prince who does the kissing—not the men-of-goodwill who do the automatic biting of the apple.)

So Jesus let the Pharisees know they were not in control of anything. His Father was. Theirs was only to be grateful for his initiating love.

Because Jesus said things like this, the Pharisees, good people that they were, got him crucified. Goodness without power was an insufferable situation for them. They defied our Lord with what was, for them, an unanswerable question: "What's the sense of doing good if I can't in some way control those for whom I do good?"

The Pharisees didn't like their passive role. They reacted outrageously. They rejected Jesus, even to the cross. That is one way to mismanage the doing of good works—complete rejection of the God (or friends) one cannot control.

The other way—Snow White's way—is the more favorite procedure: fall into a coma, go to sleep on everybody (by way of drugs, drink, television addiction, hypochondria, silent treatment, etc.):

> "People don't appreciate me for all the good I do for them!"

> "Nobody cares that I'm giving 80% to our marriage and only getting 20% back!"

> "That kid has 17 years' worth of clothing and feeding and doctor's bills from me. All I ask him to do is fill out the image that I have for him and get a haircut!"

"I did them a favor once. It's time they did one for me!"

On and on go the complaints. There is more righteous indignation and justified griping coming from the goodness of good people than from any other source. Perhaps this is why Jesus preferred the company of sinners to that of the righteous ones. He found it difficult to bear the noise of their well-documented grievances. At least sinners were in the right mood to receive the grace of God.

It is easy to do good to others; but it is not so easy to live with it afterward. There is a discipline of humility that is demanded and a delicate sensitivity to the pain of those on the receiving end.

St. Vincent de Paul saved many skid-row derelicts in Paris. Yet he would pray for hours and humbly ask his clients to forgive him for helping them. Kindness brings out a superior/inferior relationship—consoling for the giv*er,* but hard on the giv*ee.*

When I help an old lady across the street, give a bum a break, offer advice to a youngster, my giving points out the fact of their need. Unless they are extremely mature (or have quit on themselves entirely), they aren't going to like the inferior position of which my kindness reminded them. Sometimes they will strike out against me, behaving defensively, for they resent my power acting on their relative powerlessness. At the very least, they will twist and turn in order not to be in my control. They may be grateful; but they will have their own ways of showing it, not mine.

There are no magic apples. Whenever good people expect rewards for their kindnesses, and get dejected when it doesn't happen, the goodness (which *was* goodness to begin with) turns sour in the soul. What starts as love changes into a manipulative ploy because of the afterthought desire to "get something out of " what was originally a gift.

The problem is not in the act itself. Most people are good—generous, hospitable, caring—in the first immediate instinct of their heart. The problem comes afterward, when soul sits back and says, "Okay, now it's my turn—what do I get back?"

This is where humility must develop. The question is: "Was the giving act a good thing to do? Then let it be done. I'll not let the left hand of reflection know what the right hand of kindness so spontaneously took care of."

This is what Christ did. The 10 lepers (Lk 17:11-19) were cared for, even though only one came back to say thanks. Crowds were taught about the Eucharist (Jn 6:25-71) even though only a few were willing to believe. Christ cares, even though only a few care in return.

This is what it means to be a Christian. All else is Phariseeism, mismanaged charity, and Snow White at her worst. We are to be like Christ—to do good because good is good to do, not because it gives us a bite of the magic apple of control.

HOW TO HANDLE A 'SNOW WHITE EXPERIENCE' — TWO

Watch Out for Your 'Wows'

This Snow White is completely different from the last one. So is the experience to be described and so is the danger spinning off the experience. The two considerations are linked together only because both deal with superior/inferior relationships that can mean trouble.

The first Snow White was a fantasy creature—a pretty girl conceived in the mind of storytellers and celebrated by Walt Disney studios. The second Snow White is a dazzling or intense experience—a "high" like that experienced by three chosen disciples on the Mount of Transfiguration. The event is described in Chapter 17 of St. Matthew:

"Six days later," (that is, six days after Jesus proclaimed the doctrine of the Cross: "If a man wishes to come after me he must deny his very self, take up his cross and begin to follow in my footsteps."), "Jesus took Peter, James and his brother John and led them up on a high mountain by themselves. He was transfigured before their eyes. His face became as dazzling as the sun, his clothes as radiant as light" (Mt 17:1-2).

What the disciples experienced was something truly marvelous. It was majestic, gratifying, consoling. They were, by association with Jesus, really "somebodies." No wonder Peter said, "Lord, it is good for us to be here!"

It wasn't much fun listening to Jesus when he promised them the cross or warned them they must let go of their own securities ("lose their life") if they wanted to find themselves in God. Our Lord's words six days before had saddened them. The challenge made them uncomfortable.

But this was exhilarating—it was a "wow." No wonder Peter then said:

> " 'Lord, how good that we are here. With your
> permission I will erect three booths here,
> one for you, one for Moses and one for Eli-
> jah.' He was still speaking when suddenly a
> bright cloud overshadowed them. Out of
> the cloud came a voice which said, 'This is
> my beloved Son, on whom my favor rests.
> Listen to him' " (Mt 17:4-5).

The transforming experience of the goodness of God and of his magnificent love made things clearer to the favored disciples; they saw how wonderful the Father is, and how much more enjoyable it would be to remain on the mountain than to go down below and return to the confusion of everyday life.

Jesus was gentle with them. He "came forward toward them and, laying his hands on them, said, 'Get up! Do not be afraid.'" But he did take them down from the "high" of the mountain and lead them back to the nitty-gritty waiting in the valleys and villages below, the way of the Cross. Love had to be proved by faithfulness. It could not simply be relished in consoling awareness.

Then Jesus cautioned them *not* to speak of their lovely experience to the others. They must keep it to themselves until all the disciples (after the Resurrection) have had their own personal experience of the Transfiguration:

> "As they were coming down the mountainside, Jesus commanded them,
> 'Do not tell anyone of the vision until the Son of Man rises from the dead'" (Mt 17:9).

You can imagine what would have happened if they went about blurting out their wonderful experience. No matter how sensitively they put it—and, at that time, neither Peter, James nor John were noted for their sensitivity to other people's feelings—it still would cause resentment in others. Three of the 12 had an experience that nine of the 12 had not shared. This automatically formed a have/have-not relationship. A quarter of the group was superior to the others in the group.

This is a delicate situation. Most people—whether they do it deliberately or indeliberately—like to "lord it over" others by a triumphant recital of their wonderful experience.

I heard a story once about three newly ordained priests who returned to their monastery after having made a special kind of retreat called a Cursillo. The retreat was a moving thing for them—a "wow." They reached a depth of understanding of the Lord and felt a joy in his presence in a way they never had before. They were enthusiastic and exuberant.

But two of them had not yet left the mountain. One even said, in the company of about 20 priests, "This is the first real retreat I ever made in my life!" Well, among that company of 20 priests were two who had given retreats to these same three men some years past. The sting of that proclamation was like a slap in the face for them. Worse than a slap in the face—it was a consignment to nonentity. It said, "You two priests did nothing for me. You are nobodies. The Cursillo was everything. It gave me all I have!"

That insult was not intended by the young priest. He was simply still on a high from what had happened and he insensitively paraded it. But that was how the words were interpreted by the "have-nots," especially by the two older priests who had hoped that the spirituality and the retreat-conferences they had given were not altogether worthless.

One of the three young priests was more sensitive to the feelings of the "out group." He also had received much good from the Cursillo. But he quietly expressed himself. He had the thoughtfulness—and the good sense—to express himself in terms of a larger perspective. He related how the insights gained and the self-discipline acquired on previous retreats had helped him to be aware of the graces he had just received. He had the delicacy and tact to thank the two priests who had given him earlier retreats. He remembered links between the long past and the recent past. In this way, other people were included in his joy. They were drawn in to his "have," not relegated to the category of "have-not."

There is a danger lurking in any "Snow White experience." Without proper handling, something which is meant to be a gift of encouragement from God (a "consolation of the Spirit") can degenerate into vainglorious boasting or condescending triumphalism:

"We are better than other people because
—we made a Marriage Encounter."
—we made a seven-day directed retreat."
—we made a 30-day directed retreat."
—we have learned how to develop our intensive journal."
—we are experts in transcendental meditation."
—we are proficient in transpersonal awareness."
—we were on a beautiful workshop and learned all about prayer from Father _____, or all about healing from Guru _____."
—we are charismatic and have the gift of tongues and were baptized in the Spirit, not just in the ordinary baptism."

And so on. Add to this list other ways that people can have a peak experience—yoga, psychosynthesis, silva mind control, bioenergetics, est, rolfing, arica, a personal growth workshop, rich understanding drawn from a gifted teacher, a beautiful vacation somewhere, a deep-felt "wow" that came on a lonely beach when the sun was setting and the sea was calm, the smile of perfect trust from a baby, your own baby in your arms . . . . The occasions are almost limitless. And no two people are alike.

These lovely experiences are not to be denied. They are gifts from God. They are reassurances, consolations, flashes of brilliant insight, spiritual adrenalin that keeps one going when the cross gets heavy. They are meant to be cherished and appreciated.

I am not suggesting that we abandon our visions or adventures. I am only suggesting that we handle them with more emphasis on quiet gratitude to God for giving the experience rather than on robust back-slapping of ourselves for having received it. And I am most emphatically suggesting (in the spirit of Jesus cautioning his three disciples) that we be much more delicately sensitive to those who have not had the same experience in the same way.

Any superior/inferior relationship brings out the worst in those who feel inferior. It makes them defensive. There are two principal ways in which we can be superior. One way is by doing good for others. This happens when we are the givers and others are the givees, receiving advice, money, care, help, support. It is easy to mismanage this kind of relationship. This is how Walt Disney's Snow White got into trouble.

The second way is to be superior by *experience.* Everyone knows how defensive youngsters can be when adults flaunt their superiority in this area:

> "When I was your age, I walked to school—10 feet of snow, unlit streets, 20 pounds of books, cold classrooms. I had it tough!"

> "I've lived longer, and it's my car and my

house and my money—so listen to me."

"I've learned by my experiences, and I want to
spare you the hurts; so let me spoon-feed
you my learning and never mind experienc-
ing for yourself."

No wonder youngsters retaliate defensively.
Nobody likes to remain in an inferior position. They
think of ways to equalize the situation. Usually, it's
in the area of emotions. They get their parents angry,
one way or another (sloppy clothes, messy hair, inat-
tentiveness, raucous voice, picky appetite, etc.).
Then the adults get angry. This is a great equalizer.
There is no longer a superior/inferior setting—all
are equally irritated and irritable.

The same thing happens whenever anyone
tactlessly displays his newly found enthusiasm in the
presence of others. A good experience is a "have," a
cherished possession. It's important to remember
that others are "have-nots" with relationship to this
experience. Demands of love impel the enthusiast to
think of others—to include them in the joy of the
experience (as they are able to be included), not to
make them feel like second-rate, subhuman in-
dividuals.

I have pleaded with retreatants to be prudent
about the way they return home and give an account
of their weekend retreat. For most of the men and
women who come to us, the weekend is a very good
experience. It constitutes a "wow" of sorts. Then the
retreatants leave and meet their families on Sunday
afternoon. What happens? So often their account of
it is condescending:

"Honey, I wish you were there to hear what
Father _____ said to us yesterday. It's

something I've been trying to tell you for
years!"

"Kids, now I'm sure I'm right about what I've
been trying to get through to you. I found
out that Jesus agrees with me."

No wonder the rest of the family gets turned off!
"Wouldn't it be better," I ask the retreatants, "to express yourself in a way that's sensitive to them? They
have stayed home, without the car, eating chili and
beans. You've been having an experience that they
have had no part in. Bring them into your experience. Tell them things like:

"Honey, I had a good weekend. I had a feeling
of peace and love something like the feeling
you had when you attended that workshop
last year. And I thought of you often, how
grateful I am for so many things you are for
me. You were really with me."

"Kids, Father _____ said something to me that
you've been trying to tell me for years. I see
what you mean now. Thanks for telling me.
Sorry it took so long to understand."

These are suggestions on how to include others in
our "Snow White experiences." One way is to wait—
as Jesus recommends—until they have had experiences of their own, similar to yours but unique to
them. The other way is to help them feel that they are
a part of your new-found, deep-felt understanding.
This way, others will draw courage from the consolation God has given you, and Jesus will be
praised for the many and varied ways he has of dem-
onstrating the brilliant vision of his goodness and
leading us back to our valleys and villages to get to
work again.

THE BAD-WORD WORLD OF *BUT*

Self-Healing and a Balancing 'And'

Before anything else, I'd like to share two little poems with you—about a bad bird and some bad beasts which rule over the bad-word world of *but*. (Pronounce Fonly with a long "o." It's the contraction of the two words *if only*.).

> The Fonly is a funny bird
> With noises like you never heard
> And claws inside to tear its chest
> And tears for eyes and gloom for guest.
> It mopes about with broken wing
> And has a monotone to sing,
> The pity-pampered Fonly Song:
> "Fonly..." "Fonly..." all day long!
> "Fonly he..." or "Fonly she..."
> Or "Fonly I, or they, or we..."

Or "Fonly you were only there..."
Or "Fonly you weren't so unfair!"
And on and on—the Fonly Bird,
With sounds that sadness has inferred
And claws inside to tear its chest
And tears for eyes and gloom for guest,
It muffled-feathers every day
And broken-wings its life away.

Its cousins are the Yes*but* Beasts:
Wet-blanketing the joy of feasts;
Yesbutting into family hopes
And changing darlings into dopes.
They snarl when all the world would sing
And ruin almost everything.
"I want your help," they say at first;
"I like you," starts their song (rehearsed).
"You make good sense" (this phrase is nursed).
And then you must expect the worst:
"Yes, *but*," "Yes, *but*... I don't know..."
"I tried that once—it didn't go..."
"I have these reservations strong..."
"I know the reasons why you're wrong..."
"You have these faults..." "We have this
    lack..."
Who can resist against such flak!
One leaves the field defeated, daunted.
(That's what the Yes*but* Beasts had wanted.)
They leave to tear up other joys
And hope away from girls and boys
And pride away from men and Mses.
And life into a failure's fizzes.
They want you in their same old rut;
They cannot bear nor song nor strut;

70

Their hope is shoo-ed, their heart is shut.

Beware of beasts that say, "Yes, but."

The Fonly Bird and the Yes*but* Beasts are still powerful devils and rule a great part of our world. Both attack the beautiful and innocent victim called *possibilities*. The Fonly Bird attacks the rear; the Yes*but* Beasts devastate supply lines up front. One claws away at the past and hurts the memory; the other tears into the future and, by scaring the imagination, puts hope to rout.

The Fonly Bird, broken-winging its life away, is that tendency in the heart which mopes about with sad recitals of the past. It takes up possibilities that perhaps were valid at one time, but are not available any longer. It's one part of the bad-word world of *but*—"Life could have been so charmingly different, but...":

> A dentist: "If only I had decided to be a priest...had three boys instead of three

girls...had been a truck driver with fewer worries...had moved to Chicago...."

A priest: "If only I had decided to be a dentist...and had married...and had three girls...and had left Chicago...."

A woman: "If only I had married Jim instead of Jack...or lived 10 more years before I had a baby...."

Her husband: "If only I had studied more...or married later...or had a better football coach in high school...."

Her sister: "If only my parents were as rich as Rockefeller...or if only this one had not talked me into staying here...."

And on and on.

Such litanies do no good. They stifle the present moment and the possibilities that are actually at hand. Often enough, too, they demoralize the people around us. Imagine how Jack feels when his wife sighs regretfully over her lost opportunity to marry Jim. (I remember that my dad always found some reason to leave the room whenever Mother would start talking about her old beaus and her lost chances.)

The present is the only period of time that has reality. The past no longer exists and the future hasn't come yet. All there is, is now. It's no good to go back over the past, pretending to have made other decisions, embraced a different destiny, made fewer mistakes or more money. The world we live in is the world we've come from—with all of its opportunities taken and opportunities rejected. The many hits and misses of our past have provided us with the present we live in. Let's get on with the job, learn from mistakes, be grateful for our successes, and attend to the possibilities that are current and actually controllable.

The other danger to possibilities is the Yes*but* Beast which deadens the future. The most obvious scars it inflicts are those celebrated by the introductory poem. "Yes, *but*..." is followed by some form of disclaimer: "...it won't work!" or "...I've already thought of that and discounted it."

Books like *Games People Play* and other articles from the school of transactional analysis have noted the vengeful quality ("rip-off") of such encounters. First comes the ploy: "I want advice." The other person gets hooked and offers some advice. Then comes the "rip-off": "Yes, but it won't work for these reasons...." The "game" consists in defeating the advisor, showing up the stupidity of the suggestion. Either this is the game, or else the person asking for advice is simply looking for sympathy, enlisting pity for a situation that has the doom of failure worked right into it.

The word *but* is a killer—a killer of possibilities and a killer of whatever statements preceded it. The word *and* is a conjunction. It joins. *But* is a disjunction. It disavows, debilitates, destroys.

Of course, sometimes it is necessary to use the word *but* (or *however* or *on the other hand*):

"I like you very much, *but* I'm married."

"It would be nice to drive a luxury car, *but* I just can't afford one."

"I'd like to join your organization; *however*, my family has prior claim on my time."

In such cases, *but* is a disciplinary word. When it is a choice of either/or, *but* must assert itself—options must be narrowed down to one.

In many cases, though, *but* serves to effectively sunder what should be kept together:

"I like him, *but* he has some faults."

"She has a nice personality, *but* she's too pushy."

"He's a good worker, *but* I don't trust his drive."

"She's very intelligent, *but* she's probably stuck on herself."

Whenever we use the word *but* in a sentence, we 1) really stand by whatever thought comes *after* the word; and 2) disavow, for all practical purposes, whatever went *before* it.

A married couple came to me recently. They were talking about another couple. The man said, "They do get loud sometimes; *but* they're both a lot of fun to be with." The woman said, "They are a lot of fun at times; *but* I can't stand their boisterousness." In effect, he was saying, "Never mind their faults, I like them." She was saying, "Never mind their good qualities, I don't like them."

There's nothing wrong with this, as such. We do have preferences and priorities; and the way we normally express these is by expressing our real views in the clause that comes after the word *but*. Very often, though, the word *and* can express our views with more honest presentation of the whole truth. "I like him, *but* he's too bold," really means: "There might be some likeable qualities about him, but these are really unimportant. I really don't like him because he is too bold." The conjunction *and* keeps it all together: "I like him *and* I dislike this quality in him. He's a mixed bag of good and bad, as we all are."

And has more balance to it. *But* only pretends to be balanced. There is an unspoken bias hiding behind the apparent fairness that seems to be taking up both sides.

Two priests were asked what they thought about the charismatic prayer movement. Both seemed to be balanced in their reply. One said, "Charismatics are impressive in some ways," which he listed; "*but* they seem dangerous and silly for these reasons," which he also listed. The other priest said, "Admittedly, there are some imprudent enthusiasts among them," and he went on to give examples; "*but* the love and joy so many of them manifest surely is a sign that God is with them."

It would be better for each to say: "This is the good *and* the bad of it; and for the reasons given, I take my stand for or against." This approach is more honest and responsible. The same could apply to any discussion of friends, politics, governmental decisions, family differences, whatever. Use the word *and* to "let it all hang out." The word *but* dismisses too abruptly whatever statements came before the killer.

A Suggestion for Self-Healing

This is the most important part of the present chapter. Self-devastation is the worst of the bad-word world of *but*. I have heard many variants of "I'm no good" statements coming out of this bad world: "Yes, I am kind to people, often helpful, popular with fellow workers, patient at times—*but* I'm impatient, too; *but* I'm selfish sometimes; *but* one of my bosses doesn't like me; *but* I'm not perfect."

75

So often the word *but* destroys the goodness that a person is and does. The hurt is self-inflicted. Then, often enough, the hurt fans out. Jesus said, "Love others as you love yourself." This is, frequently, just what we actually do—we can't stand ourselves (because we've been concentrating on the bad side of ourselves); so we treat others the same way. We start out with the statement: "I have some good qualities, *but* they don't count because of these flaws." Then we treat others the same way: "They might have some good qualities, *but* they aren't perfect either—so they are relegated to the 'no good' conclusion, too!"

The way to self-healing (and from self-healing, other-people-healing) is to keep together the whole mix of good and bad. Replace *but* with the word *and*: "I am patient *and* impatient, kind *and* selfish, joyful *and* depressed, liked *and* disliked," etc.

This way, we will be rescued from the demoralizing process that concludes with an "I'm no good" attitude because all is not perfect. We will learn to appreciate better, and to develop more confidently, the good side of our personality.

One advantage of the "I am both good *and* bad" attitude is that we have a better place from which to work. Possibilities for self-improvement open up. We can, without panic or depression, take a good look at the selfish side of our behavior and do something about it. We can understand that some unhappy situations are caused by circumstances outside our control. We can then develop ways of coping with them, which is better than wringing our hands, spending unhappy hours in the fruitless wish that "they" would change.

Because it's no longer an either/or question ("I am either perfect or I'm no good at all"), we can calmly investigate what the elements are that change us from behaving well to behaving sinfully, and what the qualities are that change us back again from bad to good. Then we can manage our lives with more control, asking the less dramatic, more workable question: "How can I improve myself and help others, little by little?"

A further way of using the healing word *and* is in the area of other people's approval or disapproval. The bad-word world of *but* demands 100 per cent:

> "I do get along with most of my fellow workers; *but* Charlie can't stand me, so is it any wonder that I'm unhappy all the time?"

> "My spouse and I are doing fine most of the time; *but* he/she criticizes me about this one thing. Once a week we quarrel. So what's wrong with our marriage?"

The joining word *and* interprets these situations with a more conciliatory and inclusive attitude. It delivers us from death-dealing discouragement:

> "Well, if nine fellow workers like me and Charlie despises me, that doesn't mean I'm no good. Nine out of 10 is a fair average. I'll accept dislike from some and won't let it keep me away from the joy of the friends I have."

> "One day out of seven means that on six of seven days my spouse and I are doing fine. Eighty-five per cent is a good average. Maybe the good days can help us heal the bad ones. I'll not deny the happiness we have, just because there's still room for im-

provement in both of us."

The healing ways of the word *and* is another aspect of Christ's "sun and rain" commandment of love. God the Father does not hurl the word *but* at people. ("I'll send you my sun and rain if you are good, *but* not if you are bad!")

God gives sun and rain to honest *and* dishonest people alike. And so must we. And we will, if we *and* the world we live in. But we won't if we *but* it to death.

KEEP IT COMPLICATED, KID!

Simplicity Sometimes Does Disservice

Because I want to make an example of myself, please permit me the space of one page to slide off the kitchen stool and pretend I'm a very heavy-worded lecturer. I'd like to make some fancy talk about the discomfort caused by fancy talk.

The United States Army—I think it is the Army—has a banner advertising KISS. The letters stand for "Keep It Simple, Stupid!" It enjoys wide appeal among communication experts. It advocates the avoidance of technical jargon and obtuse phrases. It warns against the proliferation of complex ideas and intricate terminology, insisting that such ponderous presentations severely weaken the chances for any message to be effective.

It urges that people say what they mean in a simple, straightforward way. It challenges specialists, social scientists, teachers, lawyers, doctors, repairmen, writers of insurance policies and of bishops' letters to quit obfuscating the issue. It hopes that people find better words than *obfuscation* and *proliferation* (I'm guilty, too); that when Logan Airport wants employees to quiet down they will *say* quiet down, not "observe noise abatement procedures"; that teachers tell parents their child flunked, not that he's been "recycled" or "retained"; that all of us say what we mean to say as simply as possible.

I am all for it! I stand with one foot firmly under the banner of KISS. Indeed, that is why I decided to write this book. I wanted to communicate important things in the normal way most people do when they talk around a kitchen table—without lecture-hall pedantry or pulpit oratory. I don't like the name *stupid* applied to anybody. But I do take the other three words to heart: serious matters should be discussed in a language that is least likely to be tiresome or misunderstood on the receiving end.

This is one stand I firmly take—upon *one* foot, because the KISS approach is good only in certain respects. There is another banner I wave, too. I've given it a name: KICK ("Keep It Complicated, Kid!").

I take my stand under this slogan even more emphatically. True, one is directly opposed to the other. But, while a KISS is a good way to handle affection and communication, we would do well to put up with KICKs in the areas of friendship, philosophy and religious understanding. Let me explain with some examples.

Years ago in the seminary, I was one of many Passionists studying St. Paul's Epistle to the Romans. During recreation we were in a long and heated discussion, still warm from the interesting class lecture. The brother who cooked for the monastery was with us, and he was bored. He didn't *say* he was bored. He said, "Look, friends, will you please tell me, in a nice simple sentence—without any adornments or phrases that keep going on and on—just *what* St. Paul was talking about?" We replied, "Yes, we'll do this if you will tell us, in one simple sentence—without any detailed elaborations—just what your responsibilities are as the cook here."

He said, "I can't do it in a sentence. I've got to order, arrange diets, meet with salesmen, check for bargains, plan menus, etc." We then responded, "If you won't grant us the complicated nature of what we love, we won't allow for the complexities of what you love."

Jesus said: "Where your treasure is, there your heart is also" (Mt 16:21). It could be paraphrased: "Wherever your interest is, there you will be patient with complexity." Brother cook was not interested in St. Paul's theology. He wanted to get away from this subject ("Keep it simple!"). He was avidly interested in his work, and knew the importance of it, and so he was appreciative of, even fascinated by, its varied demands and rich complexity.

I know of a married couple who loved each other well—*except* for two areas of complexity. Area 1: The husband was not handy around the house. The lawn, for instance, could go unnoticed for weeks. He was an excellent basketball coach. So, predictably

81

enough, he was an advocate of "keep it simple" when it came to the home; yet he was a patient perfectionist on the court—rich with knowledge about intricate weaves, fast breaks, pivot plays, second and third options and a thousand more minute realities that gave him winning teams. He could spend hours developing the flow of one youngster's foul-shooting style; he found it difficult to spend half an hour cutting grass.

Area 2: The wife kept the home running smoothly. She was patient with details, capable of balancing all the many-faceted demands of domesticity—a competent juggler of tasty meals, bills, transportation for the kids, school responsibilities, laundry, water leaks, discount sales, etc. She loved it all. Because she loved it, she was an able "complexionist" in this area. But she cared little for sports. She tended to "keep it simple" as far as her husband's job was concerned: "My husband? Oh, he goes to school and throws out a basketball and lets the boys play; and he never gets home until late and he's away a lot because he has to go on trips."

Very often, a KISS is really a kiss-off. It's a common way for one person to say, "I really don't care!" to another:

> "A farmer's life? Simple—just get up, milk the cows, get the eggs and wait for the sun and rain to grow the vegetables."
>
> "A doctor? Simple—take the pulse, write illegible prescriptions and overcharge the patients."
>
> "A housekeeper? Get up, make the breakfast, send everybody off on time, prepare the supper and spend the rest of the day watching soap operas on TV. Simple!"
>
> "A parish priest? Nothing to do all week but say Mass in the morning. Simple!"

The world we love is always complicated. Listen to any conversation among nurses, farmers, mechanics, mothers, bishops, plumbers, secretaries, even children playing cops-and-robbers. Marvel at the rich variety of things to think about, talk about and keep in touch with.

If strangers dare to simplify those areas of life we are really interested in, they will be laughed at or despised—"They just don't understand!" Simplification usually amounts to amputation:

> "Trees are nothing but stuff for lumber. So cut down all the trees and leave a desert of stumps where there once was a lovely forest. Simple."
>
> "Man is just a thinking machine. So let's live as though emotions don't exist. Simple."
>
> "Politicians (or priests or mothers or TV repairmen) are evil sometimes. Therefore don't trust any of them. Simple."

"I have sinned. So why be a phony and pretend that I'm also a good person, on occasion, too? The fact is that I'm sometimes bad; therefore I'm all bad. Simple."

We get into trouble by working out of a KISS/-kiss-off procedure in religion, too. It seems inconsistent to me that normally adult people want their religion simple: "Just tell me what I can and can't do, and what I can get away with so I don't go to hell, and keep the language in a style that a six-year-old can understand—and don't make it complicated!"

Yet, the same people demanding such childish simplicity from their religion:

    —know almost enough medical terminology to pass a doctor's exam;

    —know the intricate requirements of cosmetics well enough to work for a beauty parlor;

    —have such a patient appreciation of spark plugs, transmissions, batteries and what not they could build their own automobile from scratch;

    —delight so in the manifold maneuvers of pro football (flanker pass, blind-side block, mousetrap play, etc.) it could make one's head swim.

What is to be concluded from all this? That physical health is intricately more important than spiritual health, beauty is more interesting than goodness, cars mean more than God, the patterns of football are more lively than the words of Jesus Christ.

Isn't this the story of every heresy? In the interest of keeping it simple, heresy amputates the complex nature of God's revelation. Jesus, for instance, is both God *and* man. "That's too complicated," say the heretics. "Let's simplify theology to make God easier to work with. Let's say Jesus was God and he was only 'play acting' as a man—just pretending." Or: "Let's say that he was only a man—one of the best men who ever lived, granted—but only a man. Then we can cut him down to our size and we don't have to take so seriously his command to follow him. We will think of him as our 'brother,' not as our Lord."

God is both merciful *and* just. "This is too complicated," say the heretics. Then they choose again, one way or the other. Some say, "Let's simplify and make God all justice; then, if anybody sins, he'll go to hell without a second chance." Others say, "Let's simplify and make God all kindness, so there is no hell; we can do anything we want on earth and then 'get around' God as we used to get around Santa Claus when we were kids."

God is the source of life and health and healing; he is also the giver of brains to people like doctors who learn how to cure sickness. Heretics who concentrate on the first statement say, "That's too complicated! Let's keep it simple by giving God, and *only* God, the right to heal. Therefore we must avoid doctors as the work of the devil."

Other heretics, like some secular materialists, say, "Miracles are impossible. God has no power to intervene or heal—only doctors and sensitivity gurus can do such things!" Simple.

The Catholic Church keeps it complicated. We agree with those who defend God's power to heal in the *positive* things they say. We have Lourdes; we pray, just before Holy Communion, "Lord, say only the word and I shall be healed." And we also reverence the healing power of medical science and of others who can help make the nervous system relax.

In all the disagreements with heretics, we do not dispute what they affirm. We dispute what they deny, what they leave out. We hold on to the complicated nature of our faith, even though we are faced with mystery by doing so: God is one *and* three at the same time; man is predestined by God *and* given a responsible free will at the same time; Jesus is God *and* man at the same time; the Lord demands that we be "guileless as doves *and* as shrewd as a snake" at the same time.

It is tempting, in these and other aspects of our faith, to make it simple. Simplicity is easier to deal with. It is more congenial to a flabby spirit and a lazy mind. In those areas of life that we don't really care about, we want things as easy as possible. But we can't do this in the area of our faith, which registers our degree of friendship with God. In this area, "Keep it complicated, kid!"

Jesus knows when he is treated with interest and when he is given the kiss-off of simplification. He wants us to puzzle over his paradoxes and parables:

"By means of many such parables
He taught them the message in such a way they could understand.
To them he spoke only by way of parable, while he kept explaining things privately to his disciples" (Mk 4:33-34).

Surely the reason for this was so that the disciples would ponder over the significance of what he said.

Jesus wanted them to grope for further meaning of his messages—not to dismiss him as "just another storyteller who spoke parables to the people in order to keep it simple."

The disciples grew into understanding, keeping in touch with all the complexities of their baffling faith. And so must we. We must be as sensitive to the manifold movements of God's grace as a mother is sensitive to the varied moods and purrs and danger signals of her infant. We must be as patient with complexity as a coach planning strategy for his ball team, as a brother preparing meals in a monastery, as a hypochondriac reading up on all the latest medical discoveries.

We must be like Mary, who did not fully understand her role or the complex nature of her son's mission; nevertheless, she did not stunt herself with impatient desires to take the Kingdom of God into her own hands and "keep it simple." Mary was a competent "complexionist"—someone who proved worthy of the Father's trust: "Mary treasured all these things and reflected on them in her heart" (Lk 2:19).

DO GOOD TO YOUR FEELINGS

Healing as a Way of Education

There are more ways than one to help a person grow. I'd like to discuss three important ones. They are different from each other, yet linked together. They combine with each other. They team up and interchange roles—sometimes leading, sometimes supporting.

They are all good ways. Not any one of them, though, is a good way all by itself.

These three ways of growing form everybody's education. (For this essay, I'll call "everybody" by the name Freddy.) They can be pictured as layered things, according to whether they operate closer to or farther away from the heart.

Educating the *feelings* is closest to the heart. It has the most direct and immediate influence, because feelings determine whether Freddy wants to grow or believes he can.

Education of the *mind* is the middle layer—not quite as influential as people used to think, yet very necessary.

Educating (or training) *behavior* is the outside layer. It is the first method that is tried (sometimes, unfortunately, almost the only one). It is the easiest one to manage and the quickest way to get results when someone wants Freddy to "do the right thing."

Influencing others by concentrating on their behavior is the favorite teaching method of educators in many fields, especially parents teaching young children about medicine cabinets, hot stoves, crossing the street, eating too much candy and giving Aunt Sadie a nice, warm, welcoming kiss. The idea is to control the conduct of another individual with promises of rewards or threats of punishment. ("Do well in school and you'll get that camping trip." "If you're not nice to Aunt Sadie, you'll be punished when we get home.")

This is an important and not-to-be-neglected part of education. Our Lord utilized this style often. "If you love me," Jesus said, "keep my commandments. And (as a consequence) my Father will love you. And we will come to you and give you everlasting life." He also said that if we don't keep the commandments, we will have no company with God—and the name for this is hell.

Both St. John's Gospel and St. Paul's epistles are filled with the method of education that emphasizes *conduct.* "Behave yourself! Develop good patterns of right living! It doesn't matter whether or not you completely understand why they are important. It doesn't matter if you feel ill-at-ease in the beginning. Just do it. Then, little by little, good thinking and true feelings will flow from the behavior patterns that have been already established."

In John's Gospel, Jesus warns the Pharisees that the reason why they do not understand God is that they do not obey God's laws: "Any man who chooses to do his will (my Father's) will know about this doctrine—namely, whether it comes from God or is simply spoken on my own" (Jn 7:17).

Our Lord's statement sounds "wrong-directioned"—even unbearable—to our modern culture which places individual freedom on such a high pedestal. The statement claims that understanding of God follows *after* the living up to his laws. Many moderns think it should be just the other way around. To a friend who asks, "Do me a favor," the response is usually, "What is it? I must know what it is before I say I will." In ordinary situations we have to satisfy our understanding first; only after this will we dare to put ourselves into action.

God's demands call for the opposite procedure. First we must obey his laws, especially his law of love. The better we do this, the better we understand God, who is the source of love. We "put ourselves into action" first; then we gradually understand the ways of true love which we only dimly appreciated when we began.

St. Paul says the same with regard to morals. The more we love others, the more we really work at it, the better we can trust our instincts about what to do in a particular situation. If we haven't loved a person very much, we cannot trust our instincts. We are still "under the law."

Take the case of an insurance man at work. He is confident about himself; he esteems, and enjoys the esteem of, his fellow workers; he is aware and proud of the good service he gives his clients. He can trust his instincts on the job; chances are, he will do the right thing and give the right advice. Wonderful.

But let's say he is not this loving to his own family. Maybe he is full of fears about his children's reputation, anxieties about their present imperfections, resentment about their stubbornness at times. He cannot trust his instincts in this area. He hasn't loved his family enough. He may be clutching them possessively and *calling* it love. But possessiveness is not love. He must go against his instincts—which would be to nag his children—in this case. He must love because he has to. He is not yet free to "love and do as he will."

Indeed, most people can trust their instincts with people outside their homes. The sense of appreciation for others and alertness to service for others is usually paramount. Yet most people cannot trust their natural inclinations with their own family. Possessiveness, anxiety and the unwillingness to forget past hurts—these things are often the predominant forces within a family. These are precisely the forces that obstruct true love. So we are still under the law here.

Also, and especially, we cannot trust ourselves. As a rule we have loved ourselves least of all. The instincts of depression, self-pity, anger, rancor and the like are heavy in the heart. We cannot obey our quick impulses the way we can when we advise a friend whom we love unpossessively. We must love ourselves even when our instincts tell us we don't want to. Also, when we have wronged someone, we must be ashamed of ourselves, make amends, learn by the mistake, and keep going—even when we don't want to do this, either.

Our impulse is to quit, brood, feel sorry for ourselves or blame some scapegoat when things don't go our way. In these cases, as St. Paul says, we must let ourselves be moved by the outside layer—behavior—and conduct ourselves in loving ways, even when we don't fully comprehend why we should. Then, as we do it more and more, and get better and better at behaving, the less we are under the *law* of love. For it is no longer a law—it is now second nature to us.

The middle layer is *thinking*. This aspect of education needs little explaining. It is the normal way schools operate. The idea is to generate the brainpower. Give a person more to think about and he will grow. He will have more reasons to behave in the right way because he has the means to think them through. His imagination will be stimulated. His good feelings about himself will increase. Confidently and naturally, he will mature.

This, too, is a good method. Jesus certainly brought us to his school and taught us our lessons. Most of his parables were generators of thought. The Kingdom of God is like a farmer; a fisherman; a woman finding a lost coin; a father of a prodigal son; a mother hen with her chicks; a man preparing a wedding feast; a woman giving birth; a supplier of sun and rain; a giver of bread, not stones.

Thanks to Jesus, we have many beautiful ways of thinking about God and his grace. This surely influences our behavior. It gives us new ways of feeling about God and about ourselves. It stirs our imagination. We grow.

The third way—the closest one to the core of our innermost self—is also a good method of education. It is different from the behavior processing of the outside layer ("Do it, or else you won't get the reward"). It is also different from the thought processing of the middle layer ("Do it to get more brainpower"). This one says, "You can do it. It's worth doing. You are worthwhile doing."

This works on processing the feelings. If the feelings are healthy:

    —thoughts can come easily to mind;

    —imagination can be quickly stirred to pull

thoughts together in fascinating arrangements;

—energy coming from this can supply new thoughts with hopeful possibilities;

—good conduct and virtuous deeds can snap into action almost instinctively (like a good ball player performing intricate moves with ease because he feels good about his own ability and trusts the competence of his teammates).

But if the feelings are not healthy, thinking is blocked, the heart itself is frozen with anxiety, and behavior is afflicted with a choice (or combination) of boredom, depression, frustration, disdain or ruthless determination to get even.

It would seem obvious, therefore, that the first step of any educational system is to heal Freddy's unhealthy feelings. No sense in sending a boy off to school to learn how to think if anxieties tell him he can't learn or if depression tells him there's nothing worthwhile to be gained from it. No sense in telling a girl to behave herself if boredom has a hold of her, telling her, "What's the difference, anyway?"

First comes healing. It must, if the feelings inside the heart are sick. This is the most basic, and favorite, style of education used by Jesus. He always healed before he taught. Most frequently, he healed by expelling the devil from people who were possessed. (For "possessed by the devil," understand "possessed by the spirit of depression, self-pity, bitter resentments, the will to die rather than the will to live.")

Whether people were blind, lame, deaf or—especially—possessed, Jesus healed them first. Then, once they felt good about themselves and were "put together better," he taught them about the Kingdom of his Father. Finally, with these two experiences of support, he finished his teaching on the level of behavior: "If you love me, conduct yourselves in obedience to the commandment of love that you have seen in me. If you do, my Father will reward you with everlasting life."

Jesus concentrated on the inner layer. He repeated and repeated:

—"It is I. Do not be afraid!" (Mt 14:27).
—"Why are you so terrified? Why are you lacking in faith?" (Mk 4:40).
—"Do this in remembrance of me" (Lk 22:19).
—"The Paraclete, the Holy Spirit whom the Father will send in my name, will instruct you in everything, and remind you of all that I told you" (Jn 14:26).

Over and over and over, Jesus healed the feelings of his people. Fears took priority. He ministered to them first—the twofold fear of 1) *being unloved* (left out of friendships, rejected by significant people, not listened to, not cared about, unlovable); 2) *being ineffective* (discouraged by lack of attainment, put down for imperfect achievement, ridiculed for inept efforts, not considered a good child, youth, parent, worker, thinker).

If this was Jesus' method, it should be ours as well. The other two methods of education are good and should be used. Freddy must learn the codes of conduct—right from wrong, acceptable behavior in contrast to unacceptable behavior. He will learn these things by doing them—learning as he goes along, and growing from his experiences.

Freddy must also go to school. Unless he is helped to think for himself, he is only an automaton. He cannot grow without the means to get himself to grow.

But most important is the art of healing as Jesus practiced it. One of the most outstanding examples happened on Easter Sunday. Jesus met his disciples for the first time since he died. They were discouraged about themselves, unmanned by fear, hurting with the guilt of having played the coward.

Jesus forgave them, concentrating on their feelings. Then he spoke those healing words: "As the Father has sent me, so I send you" (Jn 20:21). The meaning was: "Go ahead, men—you can do it. Be the leaders of my Church. I trust you."

Jesus did not bawl them out. He didn't reprimand them for their errant behavior. He didn't lecture them as students who have just flunked. He worked on their depression and anxieties. He gave them confidence again. He showed he could count on them despite their imperfections.

They moved from there. They became great saints. Their feelings were healed, so all three layers of their hearts were good again.

The everybody called Freddy must be freed from unhealthy fears, relieved of oppressive anxieties, delivered from the possessiveness of sadness. Then he will have ears open to be taught and a will eager to be trained to love himself and others as Jesus did.

"Do not be afraid" is the first part of the Christian message. Modern behavioral science words it differently: "Unless there is a feeling of psychological safety among all participants, no real communication can take place."

Both messages express the same truth. We can't sit still if we are suffering from appendicitis; we can't enjoy a sunset if we're starving; we can't be taught if we are afraid, depressed or frustrated.

Once the layer nearest the heart is healed, the second part of Christ's message can take hold: "Remember that I am with you." Then all the layers join. All systems are "go." We love ourselves. We love others as we love ourselves. And we reach the thoughts of God and behave in ways that are worthy of him who loved us first, loving the Lord our God with all our heart and mind and soul.

THE LAST AFTERNOON HASN'T COME YET

The Art of Healing Past Failures

I want to make this chapter rather special. The ideas here do not apply to everybody. If you do not feel you have ever failed anyone, you can breeze right by and go two more chapters further where I deal with how to handle the hurts that happen when other people have failed you.

I wouldn't bring this subject up at all if it were not for the fact that the subject has been so often brought to my attention by men and women on retreat. The statement of failure is usually put into some form of a question: "What did I do wrong?" "What did we do wrong?" "What went wrong?" It is invariably accompanied by worried eyes and a sad, defeated face.

The itemized accounts of bad news vary, but the

puzzlement and self-inflicted hurt remain the same. "We don't know what went wrong," wonder the parents of a wayward son or daughter. "We brought him up right. She went to church with us every week. We sent him to learn his catechism. We sacrificed so she could go to a Catholic school. We gave our child our love and our values."

Then comes the final part of the story that spells out failure: "But he doesn't go to church anymore. She scorns our faith. He's taking dope and is into crime. She ran away from home. He married a divorcee and never sees us. She doesn't care about herself at all." And the clincher: "They've turned out to be no good."

There are many people, especially mothers, who will even quote our Lord's words down on their own heads and dig deeper into the doom of guilt. "Jesus said," (and I've heard so many quote this) " 'Any sound tree bears good fruit, while a decayed tree bears bad fruit' " (Mt 7:17). "I have borne a child that turned out bad. Therefore I must be bad. I have failed him."

I must say, in passing, this is an incorrect understanding of our Lord's words. Jesus was not speaking of parents bearing children as a tree bears fruit. He was speaking of an individual—each individual person—bringing out of his heart conduct and speech (the fruits of his character) which mark him as a good or bad person. The things we do and the words we say are the test of who we are: "By their fruits you will know them."

Still, even with the right understanding of Scripture, the hurt won't go away. There is a fine line between taking proper responsibility for the bringing up of children and taking on so much responsibility that it hurts. Many responsible people go too far and drape the cloak of sadness over themselves for things that are not in their control.

How do I respond to those who are hurting from the fear (or the fact) that they've failed someone under their care? Sometimes I try to be witty: "How many children do you have? And one of the six has turned out to be no good? Well, five out of six isn't bad. A baseball player is happy with two out of six. A quarterback is pleased with 60 per cent completions." They look at me with a face that tells me I just don't understand. I do understand. But this is the wrong approach.

Another response is to link them with the Lord: "You say you taught them your faith and sent them to religion classes and even to Catholic schools. That doesn't make things automatic. I know a man who was tutored in religion for three years with the best educator of Christian doctrine who ever lived. Tutored! He didn't just have a sloppily prepared class on Friday afternoon. That's all he took—religion. And yet he learned so little from it all—so very little—that he betrayed his teacher for 30 pieces of silver."

Are we to say that Jesus is a "bad tree" because Judas turned out to be "bad fruit"? Preposterous! All we can say is that the same teaching and training were given all 12 apostles. Some got it. Some didn't. Eleven out of 12—not bad. Jesus was hurt by the failure of Judas. But he wasn't crushed by the hurt. He did not neglect to love the others who were developing under his tutelage.

He didn't. But many good people do.

I have this dream about the parents of the good thief. Nobody knows their names. We don't even know their son's name. Tradition calls the good thief St. Dismas (which is Greek for *right*) because he was crucified on the cross that was to the right of Jesus.

So let's give his parents the name of Mr. and Mrs. Dismas. It is of them that I have this dream. The dream tells me that they had nine other children. These were relatively neglected. Mom and Dad weren't thinking much about them. They focused their tormented minds upon the unalterable past that had turned their one son into what they considered to be a failure. Goaded by guilt, they asked themselves, over and over: "What went wrong? Will not God punish us for how our son turned out? How can we hold our heads up in public? Where was the mistake made? We sent him to the synagogue. We taught him right from wrong. We tried to do our best. How did we fail?"

Ten to 20 years they wrung their hands and worried themselves sick and drained their energy away from helping their other children grow up with happier parents and healthier self-confidence.

Twenty years of useless misery! That is how it turned out in their case. They had foredoomed their son as a failure. He was not a failure. He was blessed by Jesus himself—the only person, on record, who was canonized before he died. Jesus said, Good Friday afternoon, "This day, you will be with me in paradise" (Lk 23:43). He is the good thief, a certain saint. But it is only for the last afternoon of his life that we call him good.

Admittedly, this is only a personal dream of my own. I don't actually know how Mr. and Mrs.

Dismas accepted their parental implications (and the family slurs and the gossips' sneers) all those years that their son was a "no-good thief." I don't know if they made themselves as miserable as I imagine them doing. I only know that many, many parents have done just that; and I have used these case histories as the substance for my fantasy about the good thief's parents.

The story is meant to be encouraging to those men and women on retreat who are focusing their tormented minds upon the failures in their past. I plead with them: "Don't worry, all of you Mr. and Mrs. Dismases of the world! You've done what you could. You tried. Don't judge anybody as 'no good'—that last afternoon hasn't come yet. Keep communications lines open. Pray for the final outcome of your 'good thief,' and go back and put your energies into the people who are with you now. Don't neglect your spouse or family or friends, grieving over the loss of someone who is not there. Don't make them feel unable to make you happy. Let them begin again to look forward to a joyful home, an interesting talk, a gracious presence. Leave the lost one to the Lord, and to your prayers, and to his last afternoon."

Then I tell them about Mr. and Mrs. Borromeo. I have read somewhere that this is their story. If not, no matter. The story happens often in the lives of the saints. Indeed, many families have the same story—a good woman and a bad woman from the same upbringing (even twin sisters); a family from Manhattan's west side boasting a good priest-son and being shamed by a gangster-son as well.

The story, as I heard it, was that Charles (one of

103

20 children) had a twin brother, Anthony. They had the same parents, the same dinner table, the same baptism, teaching, books, environment, play, punishment—the same Jesus in Holy Communion and the same opportunities to be good or bad.

Charles Borromeo turned out to be a saint, a bishop, a doctor of the Church, a writer of books, an altogether good man, "devoting all his household goods to provide for the needy..., visiting the plague-stricken constantly, consoling them in a wonderful way" (*Roman Brieviary*, November 8).

His twin brother turned out to be what we would call today the head man of the Mafia in northern Italy. He was an altogether unsavory character—the rackets, murder for hire, white slavery, the works.

What were Mr. and Mrs. Borromeo to say? Were they to brag, "Look, neighbors, look at our son the bishop, our son the saint, our son the hero. See how well we brought him up!" The neighbors would have responded, "Get off your pedestal, Mr. and Mrs. Borromeo. Look at Tony, his twin brother. He turned out to be a rat!"

Neither could the parents wring their hands like Mr. and Mrs. Dismas: "What did we do wrong? Look at what happened to Anthony. After all we tried to do—sent him to the best schools, even! God must be ashamed of us. How can a good tree bear bad fruit?"

We must respond: "Don't be saddened, Mr. and Mrs. Borromeo. Look at Charles. You did the same for him. Rejoice in this. One out of two is not bad. Now go back to the other children who need your love and generous support. Each person must go through his own mystery of grace and responsiveness to grace. All that parents can do is be present to each as much as possible, let time and the pace of God's love work with individual free will, and determine to worry only about things that are actually in their control.

I have concentrated on parents in this essay—the Mr. and Mrs. Dismases and the Mr. and Mrs. Borromeos of the world. Their sense of failure is the most poignant. They need healing most of all. Even so, the same considerations apply to anyone in the helping professions—teachers with students, priests with penitents, social workers with clients, trainers with recruits, helpers with helpees. There is application, also, for a friend with a lost friend. In any of these situations, there can be mourning over the failure to reach a student, to help a client, to be a friend to someone who is now a friend no longer.

There are four ways of looking at past failures. There are four different concluding statements to pin on lost responsibility. It could be that:

1) the failure was mostly your fault;
2) the failure was partly your fault, partly the other person's fault;
3) the failure was mostly the other person's fault;
4) there was no fault on either side—it's just

the way things worked out.

The first two cases—failures due to real faults in *you*—need a chapter of their own, the one coming up. Go to confession, learn by past mistakes, have compassion on others who make mistakes (you aren't perfect either, remember) and keep going with the healing grace of God.

In the fourth case—the "no-fault" failure—the best thing to do is leave it alone. Here is an example of what I mean by a no-fault hurt: Taking a walk one day, I saw a little girl bend down to pick two or three beautiful spring flowers. As she did so, her school books slipped from her arms and landed in a puddle. She paid no attention to the muddy books. All her interest was on the flowers, picked for her mother to enjoy.

They met on the front porch. Daughter said, "Look, Mommy, aren't they beautiful?" Mother could not see the flowers; she saw the significance of what the girl did not see: "Look at those books! Don't you care how much we sacrifice so you can go to school—don't you care at all?"

Mother and daughter loved each other. They simply had two different sets of values and they failed to understand the love that was expressed so differently. Just because a failure is no-fault doesn't mean it doesn't hurt. It hurts as much—perhaps more—than any other kind.

The point I'm making is that it is useless to fret over no-fault failures as though they were blameworthy. If, as in this case, it is a failure of perception on both sides, we can help to widen the perceptions. We can't help by berating the perceivers.

It is the third case we touched on in this essay.

You tried to help, or teach, or coach, or train, or bring your kids up right. Some did not "take." It seems you failed through no fault (no serious or deliberate fault) of your own. Well, there are other children in your family who need a living Mom and Dad—not two half-corpses who have dug their own graves prematurely.

Jesus told his disciples to "shake its dust from your feet" (Lk 9:5) when a village refused to receive them. "They set out and went from village to village, spreading the good news everywhere and curing diseases" (Lk 9:6). Don't distress yourself with a failure or two. There's too much to do without wearing yourself out by self-recrimination.

And anyway (Jesus speaks most clearly from his cross, Good Friday afternoon), who says your "failure" really is a failure? Only God can judge this. And God has strange, mysterious ways of reevaluating Mr. and Mrs. Dismas' little boy. A bad thief turned into the good St. Dismas.

Tell the grief that is presently eating your heart out over something you can't control: "Who knows how things will turn out? The last afternoon hasn't come yet."

FORGIVENESS IS CAUSE
FOR A CELEBRATION

The Art of Healing Real Failures

This is the essay that deals with real failure. The concern is sin.

It is foolish to keep carrying past failures in our hearts. But how do we deal with them? Let Jesus remind us about a certain art of healing; let the Church instruct us how to become proficient in this art.

To do justice to the art of healing, we must also speak about the fact of forgiveness, about the need for celebration, about "booster shots" for patience, and about difficulties that usually accompany the sacrament of penance.

First, the difficulties. They are real enough. They may include any or all of the following:

     —an embarrassment to expose my sinful side to anybody;

—the hardship of expressing myself just right;

—the honest concern about genuineness, usually expressed with words like, "Why be a phony? I'll only sin again!";

—the worry about the priest's response—perhaps a bawling out or bad advice.

All these are difficulties. As a result, many people neglect this sacrament and justify themselves with a statement such as, "Why tell my sins to a priest? I'll go directly to God and keep my sorrow in the corridors of my own mind and my own heart. And God will know, and he'll forgive me."

But isn't there something lacking? The nature of love and friendship goes two ways—it's not just a one-way communication. Consider forgiveness as it takes place in familiar situations.

Say you have a friend who one day hurt your feelings, insulted you or betrayed you, denied your friendship somehow. Afterward he was sorry. But he never came to tell you so. You heard it from others, maybe, or you could somehow figure it out. You know he is sorry and he knows he is sorry, but still there's something missing. You wish he would come back and shake hands. You wish you could tell him out loud what you want to say if only he would let you: "That's okay. Glad we're friends again. Let's forget what happened and start from here."

Unless he lets you forgive him, there is a lack still in your heart.

So it is with God. There are things he wants to say to us and do for us. He wants to tell us, personally, on a one-to-one basis, friend-to-friend, into our eardrums so that we can't miss it and we can't be confused by worries and fears and guilt bouncing around the corridors of our mind:

"Glad you're here. Now I can tell you—out loud—that I love you. I forgive you and I want you to forgive yourself. I want you to be free from your sadness about your weakness. Tough enough to live in the present without brooding about the past and wasting energy with enervating self-approach or bitterness or guilt. I love you now. Come on, let's shake hands, and let's make friendship grow from here."

Our instinct about God is that he is a *celebrator*. He is not only the *source* of love and life; he is the communicator and celebrator of these things, too. Forgiveness is, supremely, an act of love. Indirectly, it is a link to life—more life, fuller life, growing from the fresh handshake.

The handshake has to take place, and it has to do so with appropriate ceremony. It's no good to be sneaky or one-sided—leaving the merciful God in the dark, not permitting him to see our sorrow, not letting him celebrate his mercy nor enjoy the act of love that delights him most.

How fortunate that we now can go to confession in a way that is more personal than the way we used to go. We give more time to God's role and his responsiveness. We emphasize the active pleasure of his reconciliation, rather than our work of wading through past sins. Now we can better understand that Jesus' mercy is primarily a cause for celebration. It is experienced in an open manner, rather than performed in a place suggestive of shadows, muffled whispers, secrecy—things more associated with crime in the dead of night than with a display of top-level love given by a God so good that he sent his

Son precisely to make this moment possible.

Let us observe Christ at perhaps the most dramatic event that showed the dynamism and delight of his Father's forgiving love. The purpose of all this is to understand the Father with eyes of faith. But to see the Father, we must look at Jesus. To find out what to look for, we put ourselves into the mind and heart—corridors and all—of a man like us.

The man's name was Simon Peter. His documented story covers three years, from his first call in Galilee to his lonely sorrow on the evening of Good Friday, to the forgiveness of Easter. Peter was a good man and a strong leader. Natural talents he had in abundance and an obvious love for Jesus that made him special. But he did have faults. He was overconfident of his strength, pushy with his ideas, impatient with people whom he felt were wasting the Master's time.

And then he fell. He sinned. It was the kind of sin most of us commit—the desire for human respect caused him to deny the person that he really was. Around the bonfire, near the court of the high priest, soldiers and serving girls were razzing him for his Galilean twang and his attachment to a disgraced nobody. He caved in to this gang pressure. He denied his love for Jesus.

When he realized the implications of his weakness, he felt very bad. He wept bitterly. No doubt he told God how sorry he was as he cried all by himself, all night long.

But still there was something missing. Look where he was on Easter Sunday—behind doors that were locked because of fear. The fear was there, even though he already was contrite in the corridors of his own heart. It was not only fear of reprisal from the Pharisees. Fear came mostly from the *inside;* the past sin still had a hold on Simon Peter.

Suddenly Jesus appeared, passing right through the locked doors of fear. He forgave Simon. Our Lord's first Easter words were these: "Peace be with you!" (Jn 20:21). It was a kind of sacramental handshake.

Then Jesus put courage back into Simon Peter's heart: "As the Father has sent me, I send you." Beautiful, isn't it? The man just got through showing that he couldn't be counted on, and our Lord turned around and made him his vicar on earth.

Finally, Jesus said, "As I've supported you, you support and forgive the brethren. Treat others the same way I have treated you" (Jn 20:19-23).

There is a sequel to Simon Peter's story. A few weeks afterward, Jesus met him on the shores of Galilee and asked, point-blank, "Simon, son of John, do you love me?" It was a question demanding an unequivocal answer: "Do you? Yes or no?"

If it weren't for the Easter healing, I suppose Peter would have replied: "Well, I'm not sure. I let you down Good Friday, remember. I did deny you. I can't really be certain one way or another. I'm all mixed up!"

Peter never said those wishy-washy words. He said a straightforward *"Yes!* You know that I love you!" He was able to say this, friend-to-friend, looking our Lord right in the eye, thanks to what Jesus did on Easter by instituting the sacrament of healing (cf Jn 20:22ff).

That's what happens each time the sacrament is celebrated. Thanks to the power coming from

Christ's death and resurrection, he can say the same to us. Using the voice of the priest (there is only one priest, of course—Jesus. All others are simply his instruments so that he can get to real eardrums in a real way), he tells us to take notice:

> "Notice how I am treating you. I'm not bawling you out, not making you feel small, not rubbing your nose in the dirt, not even angry at you for taking so long to come home to me. No, I am glad you're here so that I can tell you I forgive you and tell you to forgive yourself. See, I'm bringing out the best in you and celebrating the trust I have in your fundamental goodness."

Celebration runs all through the story. Jesus deals with us the same way he dealt with Simon Peter. He was not cupping his hand and whispering in Simon's ear, "Okay, I'll forget it this time, but don't do it again!" Not so. Our Lord was making a big fuss about the whole thing—displaying the delight and the consequences of God's forgiving love.

That is what happens each time the sacrament is celebrated—delight and consequences. Yes, consequences. The sacrament is meant to be a "booster shot" as well as a celebration. Notice what Jesus said just before he left, on that Easter day. It was not an afterthought; it was part of the whole event: "As I have forgiven you, you forgive others." This was the *food* Christ meant when He told Simon to "feed my sheep." ("I have fed you with mercy and trust—now, you do the same for others.")

We also have the sacrament of Easter peace from Jesus. When we celebrate it (not just take it with a limp hand and an itch to hurry out of the place) we can gradually learn what love and friendship are all about. We can feel the healing of our past failures. We can receive the power to forget all those past denials of our true selves—all those slippages of selfishness, all those weaknesses that came from impatience or the desire for human respect.

Then, having been on the receiving end of love, we can put ourselves more genuinely into the giving end of it. When others reject us, deny us, slip into selfishness in ways that hurt our feelings, we need not act the way that pagans do—impatient, fault-finding, sulking or getting even. No, not that. We have received—and *celebrated*—the power to act differently. We are able to forgive, to care for others, to bring out the best in them the same way Jesus brought out the best in Simon Peter and in us. We are able to do this because Christ has already given us a "booster shot" of God's forgiving energy.

This is the way that healing happens. First we are loved by God. Then we take the trouble to experience it, to really let it sink in. Then we have the power and courage to love others in the same healing and patient way.

And so we grow. God's love continues to be our enjoyment and employment.

And then one day, when we finally reach *our* version of the shore of Galilee, Jesus will say to us as he said to Simon Peter: "Do you love me?" (Jn 21:16).

We will remember especially the sacrament of forgiveness, and we will be able to say, straightforwardly: "*Yes,* Lord! You know that I love you"(v.16).

LET GO OF THE PEANUTS

The Art of Healing Past Hurts

This is the chapter that everybody knows is for everybody. We have all been hurt—hurt deeply—by others. So we all need some way to heal the hurts that are in our hearts.

Let me recommend a program, starting with a story I heard from a nursing sister who was a missionary in Africa. A tribe she knew trapped wild monkeys in a very ingenious way. They took a gourd (or pumpkin) and hollowed out the inside. They then cut a hole just big enough for a monkey's hand to squeeze through. Next they threw peanuts inside the pumpkin, tied it to a tree, and left.

When all was quiet, the monkeys would investigate, smell the bait, reach in to get the peanuts, make a fist with them, and then try to squeeze out the same way. But the opening was too small for the fist to get through and the only way they could hang on to the peanuts was by making a fist. So they were stuck. They'd be screaming with rage and fear as the natives picked them up the next day and shipped them off to live behind steel bars in some untidy zoo away from home forever.

Pretty dumb, isn't it? One feels like yelling at the monkeys, "Come to your senses, monkeys! Let go of the peanuts! Your arm can get out the same way it got in, and you'll be free to swing on trees and eat bananas and have all kinds of fun. If you stay the way you are, you're trapped. You've made yourself a prisoner of those stupid peanuts! Let them go and you'll be free!"

The monkeys would not listen. Peanuts—those stupid peanuts—were more important than their life.

Very often, people won't listen either. The "peanuts" that trap people are mostly hurts—past hurts that the memory makes a fist out of and won't let go. They are called by different names—grudge, vindictive punishment, resentment over some past disgrace, or righteous indignation at "what So-and-So did to me!" Or it could be self-condemnation and self-reproach; forgiveness of self is just as difficult as forgiveness of others. All these add up to hurts lodged in the active memory—and the memory won't let go of them.

It's a strange thing about these human "peanuts." When we are holding on tight, it doesn't really matter whether we are justified or not in feeling hurt. As a matter of fact, I'm only talking about the so-called "justified" kind of hurt.

There is no other kind, anyway. As soon as a person comes to realize he is unjustified in feeling hurt—that there is not any really good reason for feeling so—he is not hurt any longer. All the hurts that are still in our hearts are there because of a good reason. We feel it's a good reason, anyway.

I've never in my life met anyone who didn't feel justified in the unforgiving attitude he has taken. Everybody is justified, because everybody has been treated unfairly, by family or friends, at one time or another.

So we are all in the same situation. We've been hurt. Our memories give us good reasons for feeling rotten. But that's not the point. The point is that we simply can't let this hurt continue to erode our energies.

If somebody put us down or did us dirt, that's his fault. God will judge him and forgive him if he is sorry. But if we keep nursing the grudge and keep touching the wound and keep feeling sorry for the hurt that he/she/they gave us, then we are still controlled by the past and the one that hurt us still has us like a puppet on a string. We are still hanging on to the peanuts, unfree and unhappy, just like those screaming monkeys. And that's *our* fault! Why remain miserable just to make somebody else sorry for what he did? It's a frightfully expensive way to prove a point—letting ourselves be trapped in misery because someone has betrayed us in the past.

I am often amazed—perhaps the word should be enchanted—by the selective focus of attention so many people have when they come in for counseling.

For such people, the present time is only dimly recognized. Current affairs and the people they are actually living with are but vague things, hardly noticed. Nothing in the here-and-now is very noteworthy at all. Instead, a rankling wound receives 90 per cent of the person's energy and I am fascinated by the specific and dramatic way this "something of the past" is dredged up.

It seems almost as if I am asked, not to be of help, but to be an audience. I feel led by the person into the back of the brain somewhere, where I am given a comfortable chair to sit in. Ahead of me is a large, indeed a *giant* screen; behind me is a well-used movie camera. The host excitedly gets behind the camera. The lights dim, the camera whirrs, and I get—with amazingly accurate commentary—the showing of a very detailed documentary that could be called: *All That Happened—The Way It Happened* and subtitled: "Now You Can Understand Why I Am Justified in Being Hurt!"

I find myself feeling quite uncomfortable, a guest-prisoner of a movie about something that happened so long ago. I see the energy—a kind of masochistic pleasure—flowing from the producer/director of the film. I marvel at how well-rehearsed and expertly reenacted the scenario is. I feel that it is doing no good—the movie house in the back of the brain is a musty place, dark, unhealthy. I would like to lead the person outdoors into the present time, where real life and good friends, and sun and rain, and people with hands and faces, are.

I would like to destroy that camera and refocus energy from past to present. I cannot. No one can. It is only that person—each person, you and I—who can let go of the peanuts of those psycho-cinemas that continue to replay the failures of our past.

At a workshop I once attended the speaker made this interesting statement: "Suicides are always committed in order to inflict pain on those who are left." This means little suicides as well—drug addiction, alcoholism, televisionitis, hypochondria, addiction to nagging or sulking.

The motive is all the same: "I feel hurt, so I'm going to let my life deteriorate. In this way, I will inflict the pain of remorse on those who did me in!"

> "I'll get sick, or have a nervous breakdown, and then they'll be sorry for the way they treat me here!"

> "I'll stay in my room and they'll worry about what happened to me."

> "I'll insinuate that my auto accident was really their fault—for making me so upset."

> "I'll flirt with somebody else, and then he/she will be sorry!"

> "I'll just sit and watch TV all evening and not say anything so they'll know how badly they've hurt me."

"And then they'll be sorry!" That's the broken record of the self-victimized victims of suicide. Nobody is worth that kind of vengeance. The peanuts are too expensive. They come at the cost of self-enslavement to the past.

Jesus told us, over and over and with frightening insistence, that we must forgive others and ourselves. We must, if we expect our Father in heaven to forgive us.

In the prayer we know as the Our Father, as recorded by both St. Matthew and St. Luke, the one phrase—"forgive us the wrong we have done, as we forgive those who wrong us" (Mt 6:12)—gets highlighted. In both Gospels, Jesus continues the prayer with a postscript: "For if you forgive the faults of others, your heavenly Father will forgive you yours" (v. 14).

Indeed, in St. Mark's Gospel, *all* prayer is summed up with that one phrase. Jesus says, "When you stand to pray, forgive anyone against whom you have a grievance so that your heavenly Father may in turn forgive you your faults" (Mk 11:25). (See Mt 6:9-15, especially vv. 14 and 15; also Mt 18:35 and Lk 11:2-4.)

Without doubt, this is rock-bottom Christianity. No exceptions, no ifs, ands or buts. Unfortunately, though, people usually think of our Lord's demand as a *law* that he laid down, and then everybody starts looking for loopholes in the law. It ends up with a statement like, "Yes, Jesus, that's a good law about forgiveness; *but* if you knew how So-and-So treated me, you would understand why I am excused from the law. You would understand why I must continue as I am—feeling sorry for myself for being hurt and watching for my opportunity to get even!"

One thing is wrong with statements such as this. Jesus is speaking on forgiveness, not as a lawgiver, but as a doctor.

A doctor would say to his patient, "Listen to me. *If* you want to live, you have to breathe. You have to eat and sleep and have a healthy body, too. These are the necessary conditions for life."

The patient would be foolish to reply, "That's a nice idea, doctor; but I personally find breathing a burdensome chore. I think I have good reason to be excused from the law." This is ridiculous. The doctor is not laying down a law—he is simply explaining what *must be* if there is to be life.

Forgiving is to the spiritual life what breathing is to the physical life. That is why Jesus made this his rock-bottom Christianity. That is why, according to St. Mark, all prayer is summed up with this necessity.

The only time that God can reach us is the present time. That's all there is, really. The past is gone; the future hasn't come yet. But if memory keeps churning up the past and won't let go of the hurts, our breath is choked off and it is impossible for God or friends to reach us. It's like trying to talk to someone preoccupied by something else. He is not present to the people he is with; he is residing wherever his preoccupation is.

We see what is at stake here. We see why our Lord insisted so strongly on this point. We must forgive, not only for the sake of those who hurt us, but also—and even more so—for our own sake.

We must let go of those peanuts and get out of the trap of our own making—the trap called rancor and bitterness and self-reproach. Let go of all those hurting memories—just let go. Soften those fists and gently pull away from the past.

And then we will be free and happy and able to live in the present with all the friends we still do have—including God, who always was our friend, still is, and always will be.

I AM NOT RESPONSIBLE
FOR SUCCESS

The Art of Healing Present Failures

Since these essays are informal talks around the kitchen table, I'd like to tell you about the times when I'm discouraged. I find it most painful when I feel that I am not a success—not able to help someone I am trying to counsel or not able to reach those to whom I preach.

When this happens, I am letting myself be panicked by a driver within me. Its name is "Must-Please." It tells me, and sometimes convinces me, that I must please everybody, all the time, in all possible ways, or else I'm no good.

Of course, only God can accomplish such a task. And not even God achieved it: He sent his only Son to heal the world and lead us all with love to perfect life. Yet Jesus failed with Judas, and with many others he tried to reach as well.

I know this. I know that I can't "win 'em all." I know it's foolish to expect to. It's foolish to judge myself as a failure if I don't succeed. Chapter 12 had much to say about my convictions on this subject. Yet I confess I don't always practice what I preach when I come face-to-face with *present* failure.

There are many examples. Let me recall one of them. Once, early in my priesthood, I gave an eight-day retreat to 50 sisters. Forty-five of them liked me. Five did not like me. (They even told me why: "Father Ike, you're too entertaining to have anything important to say!")

I should have been happy with 45 out of 50. Ninety per cent is a good average. But I wasn't happy. I more or less neglected the others and tried too hard to impress those five who rejected me. Of course, they became all the more defensive when I came on too strong. I only made things worse, and lost many opportunities to help the 45 who were available to me.

For weeks afterward, I sulked. "Nobody appreciates me. I'm no good. Why try anymore?" I had a real "pity-party" all by myself!

Why did I fill myself with such ill-tempered accusations? There was a flaw in that part of my mind which I call the "interpretation machine." I was not able to judge myself correctly. My way of interpreting was: "I must have 100 per cent success or else I'm no good!" That's what happens when I let myself be driven by the "Must-Please" driver.

I'm working at it, you'll be pleased to know. It's slow. But little by little, I'm letting Jesus do the judging: I'm just trying to do what I can with those that I'm able to reach now.

I would not have become this personal if it weren't for the fact that many other people are in the same boat. Many years of counseling have convinced me of this. A man has *one* enemy among his fellow workers; a woman cringes from the character assassination of *one* friend; a child is unwanted on *one* occasion—and the wronging *world* is the cause for self-recrimination. The person wronged has a pity-party and comes to the conclusion, "I'm a failure!"

Along with the "Must-Please" driver there is another variation—the "Be-Perfect" driver. This driver delivers ultimatums such as: "Unless I am perfect as a spouse, a worker, an athlete, an answer man, a helper, a friend—I'm not okay!"

People afflicted with this driver have many ways of putting themselves down:

> "I'd do anything to get Uncle Jim to stop drinking. I can't do it. What's wrong with me?"

> "What can I do to get my child interested in serious matters? I keep trying and failing!"

> "I wanted so much to be a success in life. Yet here I am, 48 years old, and what have I really accomplished?"

The problem—with either the "Must-Please" or the "Be-Perfect" driver—is a problem of judgment. We cannot accurately assess our own worth. Our interpretation machine is out of whack.

The answer lies elsewhere. It has been given us by Jesus Christ. He has told us enough times: "Do not judge. Do not judge. Do not judge."

He is judge. He has already told us how he will

go about it. In Chapter 24 of St. Matthew's Gospel he spells it out. The Last Judgment at the end of time (and the particular judgment for each of us) is most vividly foretold.

What are the considerations that he uses to arrive at a fair trial? The amassing of evidence does not seem to be concerned with faith or obedience to the commandments. These things are assumed to be important; but they are not mentioned as being actually calculated at the time. It is *love versus insensitivity to others* that is the singular set of weights used to tip the balance between blessedness and condemnation.

Jesus will be judge. Nobody else. The Last Judgment will be a social affair. Jesus will allocate the blessed and the cursed into two separate groups (as a shepherd separates sheep from goats). He will ask some simple, practical, homespun questions that demand, on our part, a summary response of *yes* or *no:* "Did you love other people, caring for them when they needed you?"

Our lives—the *accumulated* pluses or minuses of our whole lives—will give the answer. Contingent upon the answer will fall the judgment from our Lord's lips:

> Either: 1) "Come. You have my Father's blessing! Inherit the Kingdom prepared for you from the creation of the world" (Mt 25:34).
>
> Or: 2) "Out of my sight, you condemned, into that fire prepared for the devil and his angels!" (v.41).

Jesus then lists six criteria, or "proofs," for the judgment that he makes. They could be called Exhibits A, B, C, D, E and F. Then the case rests.

Exhibits A through E seem to proceed along one

line of deliberation. Exhibit F seems to be something else entirely.

The first five that tip the scales in favor of everlasting happiness are all success stories. Hollywood would call them happy endings:

A) "I was hungry and you gave me food" (Mt 25:35).
You can see the contented face filling with good nourishment—perhaps the belly rounding, ever so little, and the back relaxing.

B) "I was thirsty and you gave me drink" (v. 35).
You, the donor, can see the throat ripple in its enjoyment; you can hear the lips smack.

C) "I was a stranger and you welcomed me" (v.35).
You can see the way contentment is replacing shyness as some stranger, like Oliver Twist, is invited to "consider himself at home, consider himself part of the family."

D) "I was naked and you clothed me" (v.36).
Another success that is surely obvious to all. Scene one: shivering nakedness; scene two: warm, comfortable, attractive clothing. What a difference!

E) "I was ill and you comforted me" (v.36).
Again, there is an obvious change in the person being helped. The words of encouragement, the fluffed-up pillow, the news from home, the chicken broth, whatever. There was loneliness and pain before you came; there is now comfort. You may not have brought about a miracle of healing; but you did cause happiness by your act of mercy. And you can see that you did.

F) "I was in prison and . . . "(v.36).
Now, following the same mode of success story, Jesus should have concluded, " . . . you got me

129

out of prison"; or " . . you obtained a governor's reprieve"; or " . . . you hired *Mission Impossible* to plan the neat escape." But he didn't say any of these things. No happy ending here. The words are: "I was in prison and you came to visit me" (v.36).

There is no change. Visiting hour is over and the prisoner is stuck in the same steel cage. You effected nothing. You changed nothing. You were not successful. All you did was show that you cared.

Exhibit F contains what are perhaps the most consoling of all the words that Jesus spoke. Of course, our Lord is talking about everyone when he mentions "little ones"—"I consider all the things you do for needy people as having been done, personally, for me. So, when you see a person hurting from:

    —lack of self-confidence (hunger);

    —lack of approval (thirst);

    —anxiety about acceptance (a stranger);

    —obvious imperfection (naked to fault-finding observers);

    —sickness in heart or mind or body,

and you cause a change in the person suffering from whatever need, I consider such kindnesses as having been done for me. I will bless you with happiness that will never end."

Then our Lord continues. There's one more in his list. Don't miss it:

    "You don't have to be a success to earn my blessing. Whenever you notice a needy one in prison and you show that you care, you earn my blessing.

"There are many kinds of prisons. The ones that people make in their own minds are much more formidable than iron bars—the shell of self-pity, the despair of failure, the dedication to sadness or a grudge, the abdication of life's hope which is the essence of drug addiction, alcoholism, compulsive eating or wagering or smoking or any other ways people have to entrench themselves inside the steel cage of their own construction.

"You would do anything to get them out of prison—to cheer them up, to heal their self-punishing hurts, to give them hope again, to get them to say 'yes' to life once more. But you don't seem to be able to do the job. They stay in their sulks, or in their cups, or in whatever compulsion. And you are powerless to help.

"Don't think you have failed them, or me, just because you haven't been successful. You did visit 'me' in prison, even though you didn't help 'me' to get out. I love you for the care you had. It is your patient kindness that I look for—not necessarily your success."

These are consoling words. They are the basis for the art of healing the hurt that comes from present failure—from feeling powerless to help someone you want so much to help but can't, because the someone doesn't yet want to be helped, or doesn't want *your* help.

Don't give up on him or her. Keep caring and do not get discouraged. Perhaps the addict or tantrum-thrower will hit bottom someday. Then he will be ready to listen to plans for escape from prison. Meanwhile, remember (make a sign and tape it to your bathroom mirror): *I am not responsible for the success or happiness of anyone.* I am only responsible for having cared and tried, and for the fact that I still do care and still visit the needy "other Christs" in prison.

The other side of the coin—where the scales of judgment tilt down—is weighted with the word *neglect.* Exhibits A to F are all the same. Jesus identifies with the people suffering from needs of every kind. He reacts strongly to unnoticed opportunities, impatient "write-offs" or callous refusals to care: "I was hungry, thirsty, shy, naked, sick, caged— physically or psychologically—and you did not care. You gave up on me and washed your hands of me and did not care! Because of this, I have no choice: You have condemned yourself to the place where there is no care for anyone—where you will nurse your selfishness forever.

"As for the others—those who, for the most part, cared about people (even though not always successful in their attempts to help)—they will be forever happy in the Kingdom where kindly love is understood, enjoyed and celebrated."

The scene, perhaps, will be something like the showing of Saturday's football game on the next Monday afternoon. Coach and players are sitting down, all together. The game is over. This is the time for true evaluation of the past. The coach doesn't say much. He doesn't have to. The evidence is right there. Everybody watches, judging for himself how well or badly the game was played.

In the Last Judgment, of course, the "game" is our life—the whole thing—play by play, incident by incident, event by event, kindness by kindness (or

132

unkindness by unkindness). There won't be any hurry. Eternity will last forever. We'll see it all and tally up.

Jesus will not have to say too much—no more than he said he would in Matthew's Gospel. All will be quite obvious then, as obvious as football players watching, in slow motion, what they tried to do or what they slipped up on. We will say either:

    1) "Yes, for the most part, I did care. I did respond to the challenges of love as these came my way. Here is where I belong—with you, Jesus."

    Or: 2) "It's obvious I don't belong here. Send me down where hate and rage and 'every man for himself' is the name of the game."

The rest is mystery. No one knows exactly how we will experience the final judgment. But there is no doubt about the *fact* of it. We also have clues as to how it will happen and motives to prepare ourselves for this most eventful time of our eternity.

Since we already know how the scales will be loaded, it would be foolish for us not to weigh them in our favor. No furiously impossible tasks are required, but quite ordinary things—kindness, unselfish caring, sensitive alertness to the needs of other people, healthy resistance of the temptation to disgruntlement or despair.

If we keep trying to live up to such a possible and practical ideal, we will be able to think of our final judgment as an experience that we can anticipate with joyful relish instead of dread. Not only this— we will also be able to noticeably improve the grade of happiness in the world where we're trying to work all this out.

'THE HELL OF INFECTED *NYAAHS*'

Don't Let the Devil Keep You Down

I love our Holy Mother, the Catholic Church. I love, among other things, the realistic way she puts important truths together. There is drama in her selection and economy in her words.

Take, for example, the readings she places at our disposal for the fifth Sunday of the year, B cycle. Drama at its best! Jesus, in the weeks before this, has been mustering his power for the life-against-death confrontation with the devil:

> "There appeared in their synagogue a man with an unclean spirit that shrieked, 'What do you want with us, Jesus of Nazareth? Have you come to destroy us?' " (Mk 1:23-24).

It was the same complaint always made by the demonic power raging inside the hearts of people

possessed: "Leave me alone! Let me be!"

As the Gospel for the fifth Sunday begins, we see Jesus ministering in an especially thoughtful way. It was during his "lunch break." Simon Peter's mother-in-law was sick. Jesus "grasped her hand, and helped her up, and the fever left her" (Mk 1:31).

Then (almost as if to say, "That was a nice meal. Thanks. Well, now, back to work.") Jesus made himself available to all who needed him: "Those whom he cured, who were variously afflicted, were many, and so were the demons he expelled" (Mk 1:34).

There were various afflictions—blindness, leprosy, deafness, physical paralysis of all kinds. But the concentration of his healing power was directed to *psychic* paralysis of people who were possessed.

Healing other sicknesses was relatively easy. The lame and the blind did not "give him a hard time." They wanted to be healed. But those possessed by the devil were furiously against the whole idea of healing. Our Lord had to confront before he cured. It was more of a challenge. It was more of a *sign*, too. There it was that the battle really raged: Jesus against the devil—the spirit of life against the spirit of death—hopeful *yes*, defending the world of possibilities, contesting defiant *no*, wanting to be left alone to brood over its miseries.

Who were these possessed people dotting the countryside of Galilee 20 centuries ago? Were there so many of them then? Are there so few now? Were they as weird as Hollywood makes them out to be—with rolling eyes and frightening sounds and such a stench that seasoned surgeons back away, and awesome strength to make grown men no more formidable than little dolls? Not necessarily. Books and movies have such a tendency for the spectacular they tend to stretch reality away from any ordinary understanding.

That is the unfortunate part of it. We do not recognize the devil for his weirdness. Yet the Church does. She is much more realistic than Hollywood. She understands that all people are in need of the healing art of Jesus. She lets this need be known in the dismal list of woes expressed by the poet Job.

Job bemoans the dreariness of life with words that speak for the clutch of sadness of everybody, of every age:

"Is not man's life on earth a drudgery?
    Are not his days those of a hireling?
He is a slave who longs for the shade,
    a hireling who waits for his wages.
So I have been assigned months of misery and
    troubled nights have been told off for me.
If in bed I say, 'When shall I arise?', then the
    night drags on; I am filled with restlessness
    until the dawn.
My days are swifter than a weaver's shuttle;
    they come to an end without hope.
Remember that my life is like the wind; I shall
    not see happiness again" (Jb 7:1-4,6-7).

What annoys Job is not the least bit extraordinary. Nothing here suggests a Hollywood spectacular replete with fearsome shrieks, putrid odor, the strength of a fanatic in the throes of hate.

The devil is a very familiar associate of us all, like a pair of old shoes. The devil of discouragement has been guest, quite often, around our kitchen tables ("My days are swift—they come to an end without hope"). More than once, he has been our bedfellow as well ("The night drags on—I am filled with restlessness until the dawn"). If being possessed means "letting the devil do our speaking for us," we have been possessed many times—for we have, many times, let the mood of gloom declare, "I shall not see happiness again."

A high-school girl, some years ago, wrote something similar. It is almost as well expressed as the poetry of Job. It came to me as homework that I gave, after school, for students on retreat. It was her answer to this question: "Everybody has a problem—what's yours? How many ways can you think of to solve it?"

> The girl responded: "My problem is myself. I
> don't like myself. I'm always making a mess of
> something, somehow. Solution: I can start
> looking for my good qualities (if I can find
> any). I can remember that other people are
> having trouble, too. And I can always remem-
> ber that God made me, and I have no right to
> throw it all back at him and say, 'Can't you do
> better than that?' "

Job had sleepless nights and dreary days. In the turbulence of his misery he declared, "I shall not see happiness again." The girl could not find one good thing to say in her favor. Apparently, all the reports from family, school and friends concentrated on the bad side of her conduct and character. She summed up herself as a dejected and rejectable "maker of messes"—a problem to herself.

In the cartoon strip "Peanuts," Linus is warning Charlie Brown's kid sister, Sally, "I think you should stop saying 'nyaah, nyaah, nyaah' to Charlie Brown. Those 'nyaahs' can hurt."

Sally retorts, "Oh, don't be ridiculous!"

"Well, they do hurt," Linus insists. "Those 'nyaahs' can get down in your stomach and really hurt."

"You're crazy!" Sally says. "A few 'nyaahs' can't hurt anybody!"

"They can," Linus concludes. "They can—if they become infected."

Perhaps all three examples can serve as a model of how everybody gets possessed, now and then, by the devil of discouragement. All we have to do is stretch out the moments of Job's impacted misery, the girl's messy self-portrait and Charlie Brown's "infected nyaahs"; stretch them beyond imagination to include eternity—and we have some idea of what hell will be. All we have to do is force the despair past any reach of hope; draw the gloom down over our eyes and heart; refuse to be consoled; resist anyone "pulling us out of it"—and we can sense the meaning of hell.

There is a saying, "All hell let loose." But hell doesn't "let loose"—it shrivels, selfishly "uptight."

You've seen people—so have I—who have committed themselves to a living hell already. A hurt, a loss, a cluster of "infected nyaahs" has really got them down. They are so down they don't want to get up. They just don't want to. Their only occupation is to nurse their wounds—rub their grief until it gets inflamed—justify the hate-full grudge they have against the ones who hurt them, tricked them, jilted them, or simply left them hanging.

Try—just dare to try—to get them out of the bitterness that holds them fast. Try smiling or sharing something humorous that you thought might cheer them up, and watch their scorn turn your smile into ice. Just try saying, "I know it's difficult, but I still love you. There is hope for tomorrow. You have gifts and talents and many friends. Don't throw them all away."

Just try it, and you will be confronted with the same response that Jesus faced when he came upon people possessed with an unclean spirit. They will brush your hand away, resenting and resisting the hope implied in your words of comfort. They will respond with either sullen silence or bitter rage that spits out, "Leave me alone. Let me be in my misery. Do not torment me with possibilities like hope or love or life renewed! I've dedicated myself to staying to myself—alone and unconsoled. The 'nyaahs' of the people who hurt me and tricked me and pointed out the mess I was making—these 'nyaahs' have so infected me that I cannot think of anything else but the rancor and remorse that is in my heart.

"Indignation is eating me up like a worm, undying. Anger and self-pity burn in me like a fire that won't go out. I am nothing but this all-consuming thought of having been let down. So I will stay down. Neither God nor any friend can do a thing for me. Ideas like light and love and hope and life—these very ideas are the most repulsive things imaginable. Leave me alone. Let me eat of my bitterness. I am committed to despair!"

Surely you have met people who shrugged away your kind offers of consolation. It's very likely you have done some shrugging, too. I have. Thank God we didn't stay in our sulks too long—or at least I hope not. "Too long" is hell.

God does not condemn anyone to hell. The people who are there have, with deliberate and resolute decisiveness, committed themselves to be there. They have ignored God's warm invitation to be part of a Kingdom where words like care and love and kindness and life and gratitude are coinage. A world where such qualities exist is precisely what they find intolerable. The pride of wounded feelings is stronger than the hope of coming back to life again. Messengers of God's good news are greeted with an icy stare, a history of justified resentments, an unforgiving rage, an eternally interminable "hummph!"

Such is hell. It is a place and a state of mind—fixed and inflexible—that prefers selfish brooding over hurts to happiness under any conditions. It is a cruelly vindictive singing of an old Ziegfeld song:

"I'd rather be blue, thinking of you,
I'd rather be blue over you,
Than be happy with somebody else."

What can we do to keep away from that terrifying place? For one thing, we can let our friends and family exorcise us when we are feeling the way Job did. If an exorcist is someone who heals a person suffering from demonic possession, and if the common garden-kind of possession is succumbing to discouragement, people can be exorcists in many simple, ordinary ways. All we have to do is let them cheer us up, help us face life again, make it possible for us to jump out of the sulk of depression.

People are available for this. They can heal us with the healing power of Christ. And every time we let them, we are doing better than the people possessed in Galilee. We are not saying, "Leave me alone, Jesus of Nazareth. Have you come to destroy us?" (Lk 4:34). We are making it easy for our Lord to be of service.

I am not suggesting that we jump with joy all the time. Such antics would be dishonest. I am suggesting that we let friendly care and new possibilities gently pull us out of the pit of self-pity. This is much better than letting "infected nyaahs" take over the whole system.

Also (and most of all) I am suggesting that we let Jesus touch us with his light and love and programs for life renewed. The mean streak in our system is the devil's doing. He is sovereign over the kingdom of death and despair. We must escape from his hold as quickly as possible.

Remember what the high-school girl remembered. Even though hurts have infected the heart and we feel that we shall not see happiness again,

> "We can always remember that God made us
> and (whether we feel like it or not)
> we have no right—
> we simply *do not have the right*—to throw it all
> back at him and say, "Can't you do better
> than that?"

HEAVEN—AND WHAT
ISN'T THERE

A Negative Approach to a Positive Position

There are many jokes told about heaven. Here is one of them. A priest once asked the children, "Who wants to go to heaven?" All raised their hands except one boy in the back. The others pointed him out to the priest, who asked, "Why don't you want to go, Jimmy?" "Ah!" the boy replied. "You'll hafta be in church all day!"

Crude as it is, young Jimmy does express the more popular notion of what heaven will be like. But ideas of what heaven is really like can only be guesswork. No one ever went there and came back—no one, that is, except Jesus. He is the only person who knows, firsthand, both worlds. He did drop some clues—only hints, but at least they are something.

At least we know that activity in heaven cannot

be compared to boring afternoons in church or lazy posturings of piety. Jesus always spoke of his Father in terms of happiness and life and having a big party with friends who obviously enjoy his company.

Christ's favorite hint of heaven was a wedding feast. In Galilee of 20 centuries ago (and, to some extent, even now), a wedding feast "brings out the best in people." Grudges are forgotten; worries are left at the door; quarrelsome words and sad faces are no-no's. The atmosphere breathes joy, appreciation of everyone present, friendship, a kind of spirited dedication to make the feast a most memorable one.

Jesus could get no closer than this in describing, positively, what heaven will be like.

He concentrated more on the negative side—on what heaven *won't* be like. These, too, are only clues; but they do give us some idea. The clue that is my favorite is placed in Chapter 16 of St. John's Gospel. Our Lord, at the Last Supper, was trying to get his disciples to cheer up. They were disconsolate at the thought of his going to his death. "The Lord is leaving us and we do not know where he is going."

"Do not let your hearts be troubled," Jesus pleaded with them. "I am indeed going to prepare a place for you. And then I shall come back to take you with me, that where I am you also may be" (Jn 14:1-3). "All this I tell you that my joy may be yours and your joy may be complete" (Jn 15:11). "I shall see you again; then your hearts will rejoice with a joy *no one* can take from you" (Jn 16:22, italics added).

Negatively put, this is what heaven will be like—a place where joy will be so securely ours that nobody or nothing can take it away. So all we have to do is itemize the thousand-thousand things that replace joy with worry, hurt, guilt, anger or frustration, and these things will not be there.

I recently asked a class of first-grade boys and girls what took joy away from them. Here is a partial list:

- —Rain spoils my fun.
- —My mother spanks me.
- —I can't go camping.
- —My pet gets loose.
- —My brothers and sisters fight.
- —I'm sick.
- —I have to go to the doctor.
- —The lights go out in a storm.
- —My brother hits me.
- —I have a stomachache from eating too much ice cream.
- —I have no one to play with.

That's a respectable start. Now add a few thousand more ways in which grownups feel their joy escapes them. It would make a considerable list.

In heaven, not one of those hurts will be there. Not one! Everything that brings joy *will* be there, though, because God is the source of all that is good. Friends will be there, and family. But not the "not nice" side of their character. We'll be there. But not our "bad side," either.

Exactly how these things will take shape, no one knows. Jesus has not told us. How active will our memory be? What will we think of our past history? What will our thinking process be like? What will occupy us? How will we greet old friends, new friends?

Nobody seems to know. In fact, Jesus pointedly cut short all such conjectures. When the Sadducees tried to trip up Christ with the puzzle about the wife of seven husbands, he retorted: "You are badly misled because you fail to understand the Scriptures" (Mt 22:29). With this curt reply, he warned them not to conjure up fancies about life that is not within their range of experience (Mt 22:23-33).

Actually, there is more here than just a quick rebuff. Jesus is giving us another important "negative clue" about heaven. He said, in so many words, "I cannot tell you about heaven because it is too much for you to comprehend right now. You'll have to get there first—then you will understand."

Our Lord was not putting us off or hedging. We ourselves do the same thing when youngsters ask us about things that are outside the range of their experiences.

Even those same first-graders appreciated the fact that this is so. I asked them if they could explain to a little three-year-old the fun they have at school and during recess—playing soccer, drawing things, learning how to use the telephone, enjoying stories that are beyond the grasp of their kid brothers and sisters. They understood. Much of the life that first-graders enjoy simply cannot be explained to pre-school children. The tots will have to wait until they get there.

So it is with adults. Try to explain a first-grader some of the joys you experience—talking, for instance, for hours on end, with a friend who stimulates your mind and delights your heart, not knowing where time has gone (almost as if you had a taste of eternity). Try sharing this with a youngster. He will wrinkle up his face and give you a "you-must-be-weird" look and say, "What's so good about that?

No fights? No toys? How could you have any fun just talking?"

Then you would sigh and suggest—as Jesus suggested to his critics—that the youngster will have to wait until he grows up and grows into a capacity for such an experience.

As a matter of fact, the contrast of before and after which Jesus makes is much more dramatic than adult-to-first-grader or first-grader-to-kid-brother. At least there is *some* sharing of experience in my two comparisons. Tots, students and adults are all human, with shared human feelings.

But Jesus goes all the way back for his reference point. "Compare the difference," he urges, "between the embryo in the mother's womb and a fully grown person with all his or her faculties intact. And compare the difference between a little mustard seed and the mature tree, big and branching, giving shade to the weary and shelter to birds of the air."

If an oak could talk to the acorn, it still couldn't make much sense: "Hey, acorn, wait until you die and then get nourished by sun and rain and soil. It's wonderful being an oak, swaying in the wind, enjoying the weather, letting children play on your limbs. It's really great, little acorn! I bet you can't wait to be a free-swinging oak like me!"

Doubtless, the acorn (if it could talk) would not believe the whole idea. Or, if it were imaginative, it would wonder: "How could a closed-up, all-emcompassing seed possibly have limbs? How could it sway? What is the word called 'nourishment'? In what way could a 70-pound child climb on me? I am no bigger than his thumb. That oak doesn't know what it's talking about!"

Or try to explain to a fetus in the womb what it's like to be a fully developed human. "Forget it!" the embryo would say. "I'm happy here. Warm. Secure. What more could I ask for? What more *is* there to life? You say this is a constricting prison, compared to the life you know. Well, maybe things are close in here; but I cannot possibly imagine what I'd do without my umbilical cord connected to my food factory."

An embryo, even more than the first-grader, will just have to wait until he experiences his new life before he can understand. This is what Jesus taught, and St. Paul reiterated: "Eye has not seen, ear has not heard, nor has it so much as dawned on man what God has prepared for those who love him" (1 Cor 2:6-10. See also Rom 8:18-25 and Eph 3:17-19).

Compared to what we will be when we live heaven's life-style, we are as fettered and imprisoned as a fetus, or an acorn, or the tiniest of seeds.

We simply have to take Christ's word for it that heaven is wonderful. Wait and see. You will have joy surpassing present understanding. You will experience life to be so free and stimulating that, compared to it, life in this world is miserly and drab. And the joy of your new life no one will take away from you.

If we accept this on faith, what are the consequences—the practical "therefores"—in this present life on earth? Granted that heaven will be a nice place to live, how do we get there? Do we simply "arrive" as a baby arrives, as a mustard seed turns into a tree?

And what about those "many mansions" in

heaven? Are there "zoning laws" there—with the spiritually rich living in well-appointed quarters while those who "made it just at the last minute after a lifetime of selfishness" reside in celestial huts on the less pretentious side of town? Won't there be "haves" and "have-nots" there? Is that fair?

St. Therese of Lisieux puzzled about such things when she was a little girl. Her older sister explained by asking her to fill a little thimble and a big pitcher with water. "Are they both filled?" "Yes." "So full they cannot hold another drop?" "Yes." "Well, that's what heaven will be like. Everybody there will be completely happy. They cannot possibly hold any more joy. But different people have different capacities for happiness."

St. Augustine expressed the same truth with a different comparison: "Heaven is like a beautiful, richly illuminated book. A child will enjoy it fully, as much as he is able; the texture has a nice feel to it; the colorful drawings are lovely to look at. An adult will enjoy all that the child does—and more—because he understands the meaning of the words."

Heaven will be something like this. Each will enjoy life to the fullest, according to each person's ability to take it in. The preeminently Christian work, therefore, is to let God increase our capacity for happiness while still on earth.

The "pitcher-full saints" have more to be happy *with*. Like an adult who understands the meaning of words, these will enjoy eternities of pleasant conversation—grown-up-to-grown-up—with God and his large-hearted saints.

Isn't that a consoling thought? Whenever we are kind to someone, sacrificing our own selfish needs for the sake of serving others (as Jesus did on the cross); whenever we study the words of Christ, pondering his ways, praying for deeper insights—we are growing in God's wisdom.

Then, at the end of our life, we will be surprised. Wide-eyed with delight we will see heaven for ourselves and say, "Look, God, all this time you were teaching me to speak your language!"

And our Father will reply in words like these:

"Yes, I know.

You have welcomed my Son when he came to
    you.

You have listened to his words;
    you have lived like him.

Come up now, close to me,
    for your place is heaven now.

You have learned the *meaning* of happiness—
    now enjoy it."

EVEN IF WE *DON'T* GET ANYTHING OUT OF IT

The Mass—A Special Kind of Prayer

As I mentioned in the introduction, this essay is where the book began. I wrestled with the problem of churchgoing, trying to establish a line of reasoning which might be able to change the attitude of those who don't bother to go to Mass. I did this, "kitchen-table style," during the informal times on weekend retreats. I responded to letter-writers asking me "how to." I was met on the street by people with the same problem.

Little by little, my response developed. Now I'd like to share it with my readers. (It was only afterward that I decided to share other informal conversations—other things that I've grown to believe are important to practical Christianity.)

The problem of churchgoing, as it has been expressed to me, takes two forms. The first is directly personal. It involves the individual himself. He or she is not going to Mass and justifies such conduct by the appeal, "Why waste time and energy if it's not doing anything for me? I like the Masses here in the retreat house chapel, but Sunday Mass at my parish is a drag. Why fake it?"

The other form is indirectly personal. It is a problem other people have—a friend or member of the family who refuses to go to Mass, basing his or her conduct on the above reasoning. Retreatants would ask me, "What can I do to convince them—to persuade her—to bring him along? I've tried to talk to them about it, but they don't listen to me."

This is what I have gradually come up with. I hope it will be of help.

Let me begin by first wishing things were otherwise. Advertising, especially TV commercials, has considerably brainwashed people into a client-centered orientation toward life.

Products and services advertised on TV present themselves as existing solely to make their clients happy. The jingles for MacDonald's hamburgers expresses the spirit as well as any:

"You, *you're* the one, the one we're working for. We do it all for *you!*"

Whether it's cars or computers or sugarless gum or gas stations which promise to be "very friendly," the whole attitude is, "Our only purpose is to help you get relief or save money or become more attractive or taste life's pleasures with more gusto. Buy our product, use our service, and you'll be able to say, 'I'm glad I did, because I got something out of it.' "

After a while, this appeal becomes a mild form of

brainwashing. An attitude grows in the hearts of television viewers which presumes to say: "Product, your job is to please us!" Then God comes into our consciousness and we often treat him as though he were just another company competing for our interest. It is almost as though the blessed Trinity should sing, "We don't matter much. Our whole reason for existence is to make you happy. You, you're the one. We do it all for you."

God is thought of as "just another booth in the bazaar" of commercials competing for our interest. "And if I don't get anything out of his 'services,' " we seem to say, "I'll take my trade where I can get some immediate gratification."

I believe this client-centered attitude to be very influential in modern culture. I wish it were otherwise, but vague wishing does not help anything. However, beginning with this line of thought does help us to understand the problem of churchgoing. It is easy to see why some people who don't feel they get much out of Mass stop going. They are simply asking the same question they ask about products on the market. "What am I getting out of it?"

Also, this helps to understand why a flat command ("Go to Mass or you'll get it!") is not very helpful. It does not come to terms with the assumption that "a thing is no good unless I can see its value to me."

Rather than suggest any more flat commands or discuss other reasons for the importance of Sunday Mass attendance (for these, I recommend *Why Sunday Mass?*, edited by Karen Hurley, St. Anthony Messenger Press, 1973), I would like to approach the subject of churchgoing somewhat differently, from the point of view of justice and gratitude.

Aristotle considered acts of religion to be part of the virtue of justice—that is, "owning up to what we owe." We don't "owe" something to God as we owe something to other people. Yet we do owe him gratitude, some way of saying "thanks" for what we have received.

It is faith, and tradition understanding this faith, which tells us how to "pay our debt" of gratitude. But justice is the virtue that operates here.

Looked at in this way, it is easier to see why the favorite objection to churchgoing does not make sense. Would anyone say: "Why change my baby's diapers at three in the morning? It doesn't *do* anything for me." "Why keep my promises if it's a bore to do so?"

We do many things because we would be unjust ("not living up to what is right") if we didn't.

Acts of religion are in the category of things by which we "own up to what we owe." The "owning," in this case, is paying our dues or keeping our word. In the case of religion, it is right and just that we give thanks to God for creating us, sustaining us and loving us even to the pledge of life eternal.

Gratitude is the way we pay our debt to God. What about gratitude? How do we know the real thing from the false? What are some human, ordinary ways that a "thank you" is understood or suspected?

Let me respond with a couple of stories—true ones. When I was a little boy, seven or eight years old, I gave my mother a left-handed baseball glove for her birthday. She didn't play baseball; she wasn't left-handed. I did, and I was.

My dad talked to me that afternoon. "This was a gift, right, son?" "Yep." "For your mother, right?" "Yep." "Well, don't you think she ought to have something to say about it?" "(Gulp . . .) Yep."

That is the first time I learned that gift-giving is more than just remembering the loved one; it is also thinking of what will please the other person and doing something that will say "thank you" in a way that he or she can understand.

Another story—similar and also true. There was a high-school girl, a few years ago, who gave her mother a record of the Rolling Stones for Christmas. Now her mother's tastes ran to Glen Miller, Fred Waring—the big bands of 40's. Her daughter didn't like this music; she liked rock and roll. I suppose, if daughter were put to it, she would have said, "I'm not giving Mom a gift if I'm not going to get anything out of it!"

The mother was hurt. She didn't say anything. There was no "scene," just a quiet hurt that her daughter had not bothered to please her.

The very nature of a gift—a *true* gift—demands the shift of focus from *me* to *thee*. Tradition supplies certain occasions where the expected thing is to remember his/her birthday or say Merry Christmas to a loved one. On these special days, the gift is a sign of love and a treasured way of saying "thank you" for the friendship or family bonds or marriage vows or whatever.

The gift-giver spends some time, first of all reflecting on what will please his beloved. If she "drops a hint" about what she would like for Christmas, he doesn't mind the trip to the store, the traffic jams, the money he could have spent on himself. He's glad to do it. It is something that he knows, beforehand, will make the "other" happy—and "other" is the whole focus of his concern.

So it is with the Mass when considered as a gift, a sign of our gratitude to God. The Mass is not the *only* gift we can give; it is not the *only* way to thank him. It is—and only faith can make this statement— the "thank you" that pleases *God* the *most*.

We give gifts to those we love because of the love that has already been in operation. So faith demands of us, in justice, that we thank God for his love which has already been in operation.

How has he loved us? Besides creating us and caring for us—benefits that all religions under- stand—the Christian faith reveals that he loved us even more intimately, even more personally. God sent his Son to be born of Mary, to grow up slowly, to teach, work, heal, die on a cross for us and rise from the dead to give us hope. Not for himself did he do all this—for *us*. His concern was not, "What am I getting out of it?" His concern was the same concern all mature people have when they give birthday presents or Christmas gifts to those they love. Mature people ask, "What will please the other? What will be the best way to let them understand that I love them and am grateful for our friendship?"

Christ's intimate and personal proof of God's love for us is the basis for our responsibility to love him back. We are in debt, so to speak, to love. Somehow, it is right and just to show our appreciation. But how? What would be a good gift to be given, on certain occasions, that could let God be just as pleased with what I've given him as my brother was when he took his package from under the tree and found "just what he always wanted" from me?

In a very real sense, God has "dropped a hint"— a very big hint—about what he would like. Indeed, Jesus more than hinted—he revealed it: "Through me, with me, in me, offer to God our Father the acknowledgement of his love and the gift of your praise."

Of course, if God had not intervened in our world, we could still "do our own thing" and worship any way we pleased. It could still be a completely subjective thing as it was in pagan times. We could still bow down to the stars, or the Sphinx, or a block of wood, or a sculptured piece of granite. We could pray to God after consulting only our own selves—our particular mood or individual temperament. We could be completely free to satisfy our need for prayer by a walk in the woods, or a chant on a mountaintop, or a quiet time in a shady glen, or on the oceanside. (The next chapter deals with different styles of prayer—all of them good—depending on training or personality.)

This would be the only consideration—the subjective criterion that asks, "Is it working for me? Am I getting anything out of it?" This would be so *if* God had not intervened.

But we know by faith that God *did* intervene. He sent his Son into the world to tell us (in so many words): "Do this as a remembrance of me" (Lk 22:19). This is the best way you have for honoring your debt of gratitude to God.

"Please don't make your prayer an either/or thing—either Mass *or* the style of personal prayer that is more meaningful to you. If you like to walk in the woods, or practice Zen, or sit by the sea for hours, fine. Do so. But don't let this replace your public worship at Mass. Do both.

"Remember, love is a two-way occupation. You know my Father's love. Is it too much to ask that you love him back—that every week, you publicly unite with me to thank my Father in the way that gives him greatest pleasure?"

Of course, if we do get something out of the Mass, fine. The Church has been after priests and people to make the Mass as meaningful as possible. But this is just a fringe benefit. Sometimes the Mass really moves us; sometimes it is boring, and we feel like a bump on a log, like we're wasting 50 minutes.

Even so, we're thanking God, giving him honor whether we get anything out of it or not. Our love is other-directed; our gift of gratitude is focused on the person loved, not on self. This gift of thanks keeps the communication lines open. It signifies the hope that our life with God may continue to grow. It says, as the Second Eucharistic Prayer puts it:

> "We thank you, Father, for counting us worthy to stand in your presence and serve you."

We are no longer immature donors of a left-handed baseball glove or a record of the Rolling Stones. We are responsive to God, who is the acknowledged source of all that we have that is good, the source of time and all of our talents and love and life and everything.

This way, we understand the Mass in its most important aspect—an act of "owning up to what we owe to God"; that is, an act of gratitude. We express this act of gratitude in the way we know (by faith) that Jesus asked us to—whether we get anything out of it or not. We are able to pray, even when we're bored, the words of the Mass which the Church puts into our mouth.

> "Father, we celebrate the memory of Christ your Son.
> We, your people and your ministers,
> recall his passion,
> his resurrection from the dead,
> and his ascension into glory;
> and from the many gifts you have given us
> we offer to you, God of glory and majesty,
> this holy and perfect sacrifice" (Eucharistic Prayer I).

'MARY IS THE MODEL OF PRAYER'

Thoughts on Prayer, by Way of a Meditation

This essay is on prayer. I actually was sitting with my elbows on a kitchen table when I wrote it. No one was with me. In a way, though, everybody was—everybody I ever knew and everybody I would reach through this book.

In my thoughts on that morning alone was my love for Mary, my own training in prayer as a Passionist, remembrance of lessons learned from workshops which served up a variety of prayer styles, and a certain conviction about what I believe to be one of the basic themes of Jesus: "The reign of God is already in your midst" (Lk 17,21).

If grace (the Kingdom) is already in our midst, the work of prayer seems to be a work, not of "going out" to get God, but of uncovering what is already here, letting Jesus be more and more a part of our practical awareness. It is not so much a lifting up the heart and mind to God as it is a letting God's grace be lifted up into our consciousness.

These were the background thoughts I had. And then I prayed to Mary:

"Blessed Mary, teach us how to pray. Give us your *let be* spirit. Guide us to the present moment of our lives and let us live in it as you did.

"Every good instinct tells us the saints and artists were right about you all along. You had no 'hang-ups' about the past. There were no worries or hurt feelings submerging your ability to *be*. There were no preconceived notions about God—except that he is wise and powerful, creative and caring, nourishing and gentle. You were there—simply there—one day in Galilee. Calm, unruffled by your past, unworried about your future. Serenity was the word for you— serenity that allows for life. You were the 'good soil' the prophet Sophaniah spoke of when he commanded the Chosen People to 'Rejoice, O soil of mine, the Lord is with you.'

"Good soil you were—able to be planted by the grace of God's own doing. There you were, that day—simply there.

"And then it happened. You didn't do anything. It was done to you. God took the initiative. It was *his* plan, *his* timing, *his* devising. The Father had a lovely, brilliantly creative idea. He would live up to his promise of salvation by loving the world and leading all people to the fullness of life.

He would do this in an ingenious way. He would send his own, his only Son, into the world. God would be made flesh. This God-made-flesh would begin as a baby, so that we need no longer fear him; he would grow up slowly, so that we could learn patience; he would teach in parables, so that we could understand by means of familiar experience; he would ratify what he taught by how he healed, so that we could know that God wants to make us whole in every way; and finally, to show that all this was, indeed, the work of God, he would display the greatest proof of love on the cross. Then the Father would display the greatest proof of power by raising to glorious life this Son of God become a mortal man.

"God had this lovely plan in mind. But since it was a plan of love, he could not force anybody to take part in it. His plan could not start unless he could find a human to be the freely-agreed-to mother of his plan. He asked you. You agreed. As simple as that. You didn't *do* anything. You let it *be done* to you.

"We take it so much for granted, Mary. The whole plan got started so beautifully, we somehow take you for granted. But how terribly it would have worked out if you were like us in your responses.

"We are so often so filled up with the hurts of the past. Like monkeys, we 'won't let go of the peanuts' of our remembered injustices or brooded-over failures. If you had been like us, you wouldn't have even heard God ask you for his favor. You would have been busy running over old wounds. Or you would have said, 'Why ask me, God? I'm too shy, or I'll only do it wrong for you. I don't have the talent or the time.'

"These are the things that get in the way of our being 'good soil' for God. But none of this got in your way. You were free of brooding or sulking or getting all entangled in the past. You were *now*—you lived in the now, capable of receiving grace. Give us the spirit of your serenity, freed from the compulsive web of those hurts in our history.

"And you were not anxious about the future, either. It is inconceivable that you could have said to God: 'Why pick me? What's the catch? What are the consequences if I agree to what you ask of me? What kind of sacrifices does it demand? I like to think of myself as a prayerful person, but I'm not so sure of this dedication to your will—with you running my life instead of me!'

"It is inconceivable that you would have even *thought* such things. But we have. We've thought them, and said as much to God. We are so afraid of the future. The dread of 'losing what we have'—the threat of insecurity—is a poison we inhale, like polluted air. So preoccupied are we with, 'what will we say next, how will we get along, who will our friends be (and how quickly will we be rejected, starving, lonely, once again?). Our lives are like a record that is meant to be played at 33 and 1/3 revolutions per minute; yet, with all our rushing around and shopping and working and worrying, we set our world at the 45 or even 78 speed, and then wonder why prayer (indeed, any kind of listening) is such a nervous, jerky experience.

"Please, Mary, help us to slow down. Help us to live in the present moment, without the erratic tugs of anxiety, without the self-defeating drain of pacing our life according to other people's expectations, or our own.

"Help us to say, with you, 'Let it be done to me as

you say, my Lord'—even though I'm not sure yet what it all means. I trust your wise and gentle care. With your grace in my heart, I am in your Kingdom. Let it be done according to your will.'

"That's the way it was with you, Mary of Nazareth. And it was done. The Word of God became your flesh. And, in God's time, you brought forth the Word of God, made of your flesh, for all of us to share.

"Surely, Jesus was unique. He had a power and personality all his own. Yet the influence of *you* was always there. He is the only child of whom it could be said, literally, 'He has his mother's eyes.' Your eyes, Mary, and so much else:

—your warm and gentle ways;
—your spirit of prayer (was it not you who taught him how to pray to God?);
—your love for Scriptures, which became his by maternal osmosis;
—and all the many other ways that made you who you were—country, culture, traditions, training, family background, and so much else.

All these influenced your Son.

"And what about the little things that we have not been told about? Did you and Joseph plant a mustard tree in your front yard so that Jesus could watch it grow up through the years? Was it you that lost a coin and 'searched diligently until you found it and then rejoiced with all the family because you found what had been lost'? Was it you that rocked your child to sleep with the story about how the mother hen cuddled her young ones, safe and warm, under her wings?

"How many more things happened in the life you shared together that we can only guess at?

"Whether at home in Nazareth, with kinsfolk at Bethlehem or Jerusalem, among your friends at Cana, Jesus was a part of you—his own person influenced by your own personality.

"We are like you, Christ's mother, in a way, as well. All Christians—men and women—also receive the Word of God. We do this, not as you did, but just as surely—each time we hear the Word of God with faith, each time we eat and drink the body and blood of Jesus, who is *our* gift because he was *your* gift first.

"We let the Word-made-flesh become our flesh. He takes our personality as he did yours. We have the same power to 'bring him forth,' made of our flesh, for others to share. We have our homes, our ways of being nourished, our culture and customs, training and traditions—our own versions of the trees we planted, the coins we've found, the lullabys our mothers crooned to us—the simple joys like yours.

"We can bring Jesus forth, influenced by all these things that make up our personality and natural gifts and talents. We can, *if* we develop the spirit of prayer that you enjoyed.

"Help us, Mary. Give us the resolve to make prayer an activity that has top priority in our lives. We usually are so sporadic in this matter of prayer. When we *need* something, and don't know any other way of getting it, then we pray. Sometimes when we are enthralled by beauty, or when circumstances put us in a peaceful setting (near water, in a quiet meadow, by a lonely forest somewhere), then we can offer spontaneous prayers of gratitude. Glorious sunsets, a spectacular view of natural beauty, the hushed times when insights come unbidden, the stimulating moments of personal triumphs or peak experiences—these embrace everybody's prayerfulness.

"But prayer, if it is to be 'good soil,' must be more than this. Guide us, Mary, to your Galilee. Teach every day to have your *now* of Nazareth. Give us a hand to get us out of our holes of depression and hurt feelings. Be the good 'mother hen,' folding your serenity over our hassled nerves and anxious worries. Slow down our pace from 78 to 33 and 1/3 rpm. Help us to resolve, at least a half hour of each day, to be like you: in a silent place, ready to receive God's Word in secret and 'let it be done' to us—if God so pleases to choose that time to evoke himself from our hearts to our attention.

"Let us do this important work and take it seriously. There are so many different ways different people have of making themselves sensitive to grace. Some pray alone; some pray with others. Some say your Rosary; some do Zen or breathing exercises. Some walk outdoors; some sit in church; some have a quiet room where a picture or a candle is. Some use a sacred word, repeated over and over, to help them live in the present moment; some use the help of a holy book to ease themselves away from the gloomy past or the fearsome future. Some write down their prayer (as I am doing here); some recall a scene of Scripture and put themselves into it, waiting for what God might possibly call out from this.

"All these are good. It's a matter of temperament and training, for the most part. Even so, while we call it prayer, we really don't do the praying. We don't, any more than you did. We simply let it be done to us. For the Kingdom of God is within us. At God's initiative, and in his timing, according to his good will, the spirit of Jesus in us prays to God our Father. We simply 'get the soil ready.' Our work is to be in the here-and-now, attentive to the possibilities of God's active grace, 'sensitive with a keen and ready ear' to God's evoking his intentions up from the inside stillness of our hearts.

"It may be that we just 'waste' this half hour of each day. Many days it will seem to be just this. But it will not be wasted. (Were those years you prayed before the Annunciation *wasted?*)

"It is very likely that prayer will be more simple and peaceful as the years roll by—like any kind of intimacy. (The style of communication between a sixty-year-old couple will be different from the style they had when they were newlyweds.) No matter. The development of the style of prayer is God's work, too. All we need to be is faithful in it.

"For this, we need your gentle guidance, Mary. Help us to stay with it, resisting the tendency to put it off because of pressing needs, or to give it up because of dryness or distractions.

"Fill us with the spirit of your *fiat.* Soothe our tensions so that we can let it be done to us according to God's Word, the Word made of your flesh—and now, thanks to you, abiding in our hearts, too."

AND THE LORD SAID, 'PEACE!'

The Lesson of Patience in Christ's Parables

Our last kitchen-table conversation should have some tone of solemnity to it. It is a farewell of sorts. Something is needed to go with the final cup of coffee and the 10-minute handshake before the book is closed. *Patience* seems a good note to end on.

What could be called *parables of patience* form a substantial part of Christ's teaching. In the parable of the nobleman, St. Luke expressly says, "He went on to tell a parable, because he was near Jerusalem where they thought that the reign of God was *about to appear*" (Lk 19:11).

That is, the disciples were looking for fast answers, quick results, a here-and-now grasp of the last line of all fairy tales—"And they lived happily ever after!"

Jesus was speaking of the ordeal (soon to come) of his passion and death in Jerusalem. He knew that he was to let all people be drawn to him by love, not by force. This way of love has to be a slow process, demanding patience and perseverance.

His disciples, apparently, preferred some shortcuts. They wanted the reign of God to come immediately: They thought that the reign of God (that is, the *parousia,* or "the experience of bliss, with God's influence experienced by all") was about to appear.

Jesus wanted to slow down their impatient expectations. He spoke many parables in order to teach them (and us) the necessity of persevering, of not getting discouraged even though the world is still far from perfect.

In one story after another—almost with the insistence of waves breaking on the shore—Jesus left us his legacy in one word: "Patience!"

Nowhere is this lesson made more obvious than in the wheat and weeds parable given such prominence in Chapter 13 of St. Matthew's Gospel. It is good to remember that Jesus was not talking to his enemies. The "bad guys" in this story are really good people—Christ's own followers. Strange thing about impatience, though—it has a way of turning good people into bad.

"The reign of God," Jesus began, "may be likened to a man who sowed good seed in his field" (Mt 13:24). It was all good seed. The design was that there be a perfectly good field of rich, full grain.

The parable continues: "While everyone was asleep, his enemy came and sowed weeds through his wheat, and then made off. When the crop began to mature and yield grain, the weeds made their appearance as well" (vv. 25-26).

The curtain falls on scene one. If we take the symbols away, the story is familiar enough. It is the very stuff of history, of scuttlebutt at work, of neighborhood exchange, of conversation brought up at home, of the seven o'clock news, of all of us— globally, grouply and individually—all over.

Weeds and wheat is the story of good and bad in us and others and nations and neighborhoods. Good and bad exists together, growing out of the same soil, taking energy from the same sun, swaying in the same wind, holding on to its roots with the same tenacity. In self, family, Church, world—in all of us—there is the "mixed field" of caring and selfishness, resolution and despair, acceptance and jealousy, spontaniety and sullenness, cooperative love and callous manipulation, the celebrations of life and the ceremonies of death—the good and the bad "growing up together."

Scene two: The servants in the story notice what is happening to the wheat field. (They are as perceptive to what's wrong as gossips are; they are as sensitive to imperfection as we are in our most disgruntled moods.) They see the weeds, and *they don't like them!*

(These farmhands of the story represent us, remember—us "good people" who belong to Christ and who really care about the Kingdom.) They see the weeds and their impulsive response is twofold— impatience with the imperfection of the field and a rather impertinent blast of anger against the master who let it happen: "Lord, didn't you sow good seed in your field?"

"Yes, I did," the master replies.

At that, one can almost see eyes fill with fire, muscles tighten for a fight, disappointment in the heart forgetting to know its place, letting mouth erupt with the demand, "Then tell us *why there are weeds.*" ("What's the matter with you, God? If your intention is to have a good crop of wheat, what's the reason for all these imperfections existing side-by-side with the good?")

"An enemy has done this," is the simple reply.

Then comes the further impatient gesture. Compelled by the energy of indignation, the farmhands ask permission to destroy the field: "Give us leave, Lord, to root out all the weeds!" It is as if they said, "Trample on the imperfections! Put sickle or sword to them! Sins and selfishness have cropped up in my self, in my family, in my community—these are unbearable to me!

> "I cherished so dearly the wish that by now I would have been perfect;
>
> 'I had hoped so strongly that my children would become what I wanted them to be;
>
> "I had so reasonably expected that the Church would be made up only of saints, that fellow workers would all be fair, that people would all live up to their promises, and that love would sway the world.

And it's not so!

"And I don't like it! And I'm going to do something about it—nag the family even if it means rooting out their joy or hope in life; retaliate with violence against the spotty, vaguely functioning, imperfect plans of Church or world or neighborhood. Vent my anger! Put teeth into righteous indignation!

"Give me permission, Lord, to cut down all the weeds, and judge the world (or me, or both) as bad!"

In scene three the master appears again. He could be almost forgotten in the vehemence with which the servants concentrated on the wrong things in the wheat field. I doubt that the servants even expected any answer from the master at all. If he did answer, it was assumed that he would simply rubberstamp the decision for uprooting which they had already decided on—something like: "You're right, boys. The wheat fields of my world have most certainly gone to seed. I guess there's nothing we can do but put the demolition squad to work and give those weeds a lesson they'll never forget, even if it means destroying the whole field in the process."

I think that's the kind of comment the servants had expected. I'm sure that's the kind of thing most supposedly "good" people expect from God when they are bitter about the imperfections in themselves and others.

That's what makes the master's reply so striking, so surprising. "And the master said, *'No!'* " He doesn't rubber-stamp the servants' wishes at all. He doesn't even suggest they calm down a little before they go out with their weedkillers. He doesn't mollify with any wishy-washy comments like, "Well, okay, if you feel you *have to;* but try not to pull the wheat up—be *careful.*"

He says none of these things. He says it straight— *"No!* You have no permission to indulge yourselves with any methods of destruction on the wheat fields of my world. *No,* and that's final!"

Then, after the negative, comes the positive commandment: *"Let both* wheat and weeds *grow together* until the harvest. Then *I* will judge the good and the bad; *I* will weed out those who have given themselves up to imperfections. Your job is not to weed out, or judge, or destroy. Your job is to make sure things grow.

"Besides," the Lord continues, "You can't really tell, from your vantage point, what are weeds and what are wheat. Look at your own past. Wasn't it that miserable year (maybe in high school or whenever that time in your life was when you felt adrift and rootless) that now, in retrospect, turned out to be so valuable? Didn't you have to go through the darkness—frightened and lonely—in order to come to understanding? Yet your parents, your friends, even yourself perhaps, were classifying that dismal time as 'weeds':

'What are we going to do with our restless son?'
'Why is our daughter so unhappy?'
'When am I going to find myself?'
'What's it all about?'

"Now you see the time as the 'growth of the wheat.' It was a period of life you are glad you had, for it was then that you developed self-assurance through trial; it was then that you formed a capacity for compassion; it was the time, most of all, that made you aware of my grace 'raising you up' from your own self-stunting depression."

Maturity comes from taking responsibility for our hurts and imperfections—determining to learn from them; deciding, resolutely, to reroute the energy of our wrong-headed behavior into a right-minded course. That is how we grow, as long as we have patience. That is how we help others grow. We cannot really distinguish weeds from wheat. All we can do is keep the soil healthy and help to give the wheat a chance.

Patience. That one word is the legacy I leave in this book. It is the word I hear most often from the God of my personal prayer. It is the quality that I most firmly must develop in myself. It is preeminently the "tag line" of all the kitchen-table counseling that I have done in the last 15 years.

It focuses on the two favorite "broken records" of our Lord. Almost like a broken record, the Gospels remember Jesus insisting that we are not to judge. He is the master, we are the farmhands. Nor are we to be anxious. He has given us so many proofs of love that we cannot doubt that he will continue.

Judging looks to the past. Hurts that are still lodged in the memory have a way of infecting the "interpretation machine" in our brain. We cannot interpret behavior or personalities correctly (especially with regard to ourselves or those close to us) because our ability to judge is marred by our unforgotten past.

So we must let God do the judging. He is really better at this business anyway. We must be patient with the way (and often the slow pace) in which he judges. His interpretation machine is far superior to ours. And if, sometimes, we still feel like getting so impatient that we want to destroy imperfections (even when it means destroying the possibilities for growth as well), we must let God frighten us away from this impulse by his imperious command: "No!" Understand the words as almost the equivalent of the modern slang phrase: "Cool it!"

Anxiety looks to the future. Our flawed interpretation machine (infected by the hurts in the memory) has a way of imposing anticipated hurts on to the imagination. Memory, sensitized to the failures and frustrations of the past, predicts "more of the same, but worse" for the future:

> "I was jilted, so nobody will ever really care about me."
>
> "I got fired, so I'll never hold down a job."
>
> "God didn't answer my prayer 10 years ago, so he won't ever. So why pray?"

Here, too, our Lord continues his appeal for patience. Let the imagination think of ways to improve the "soil," obeying Christ's injunction to "let all things grow together until the harvest."

By putting imagination to work on the task at hand, even the memory can gradually be healed. Attention is distracted from worries about the possible failure of an enterprise to the actual *doing* of the enterprise. Then, almost automatically, we tap the energy that comes from past successes. Hope floods the soul, fear drifts away, and we are patiently surprised at how well the wheat is growing after all.

The legacy is patience. It incorporates the two "broken records" of our Lord—"Don't judge; don't be anxious." It summarizes the three themes weaving in and out of this book—*"The Kingdom is within us; so let's allow it to grow by giving God's sun and rain a chance to nourish us; in this way, we will be able to give bread, not stones to others."*

I read, somewhere, about advice given to public speakers: "Tell the people what you're going to do. Do it. Then tell them what you did." I followed the first two pieces of advice. The third part—what I did by this book—I leave in God's hand, in your soil, and in the way you carry words shared around a kitchen table to the rest of your life and loves.